Praise for Denise H

"[*Reclaiming Your Heart*] is an unabashed look at real life, including dashed dreams, punctured hope, and unvarnished truths that get brushed under the rug of religious clichés. This book is the real deal for those seeking hope in spite of life's disappointments."

ALAN E. NELSON, EDD,
author of *Embracing Brokenness* and founder of KidLead, Inc.

"In *Flying Solo*, Denise . . . covers real heart issues such as learning to let go, getting through grief and disappointment, and allowing God to fill that secret place in our hearts that only he can fill. Although this book was written to bring hope and healing to those who have been through a divorce, I recommend it to anyone who wants to experience an intimate relationship with a loving God through every season of life."

NANCY ALCORN,
founder and president of Mercy Ministries

"By sharing her personal reflections and her conversations with God in *Flying Solo*, Denise offers incredible comfort for those recovering from divorce and a hope for a joyous future. This book offers validation for the feelings we all encounter and a path of self-discovery that is uplifting, encouraging, and inspiring."

JENNY SANFORD,
former First Lady of South Carolina and author of *Staying True*

"In this beautiful book, Denise Hildreth Jones has given us a gift by allowing us to walk with her through the most intimate, painful, and faith-building moments of her life. In doing so, she reminds each one of us that God is most powerfully present even when he seems to be most apparently absent."

PETE WILSON,
pastor of Cross Point Church, Nashville, Tennessee, and author of *Plan B: What Do You Do When God Doesn't Show Up the Way You Thought He Would?*

Reclaiming Your Heart

reclaiming your heart

DENISE HILDRETH JONES

Tyndale House Publishers, Inc., Carol Stream, Illinois

Visit Tyndale online at www.tyndale.com.

Visit Denise Hildreth Jones's website at www.reclaiminghearts.com.

TYNDALE and Tyndale's quill logo are registered trademarks of Tyndale House Publishers, Inc.

Reclaiming Your Heart: A Journey Back to Laughing, Loving, and Living

Designed by Beth Sparkman

Edited by Anne Christian Buchanan

Published in association with the literary agency of Daniel Literary Group, Nashville, TN.

All Scripture quotations, unless otherwise indicated, are taken from the New King James Version.® Copyright © 1982 by Thomas Nelson, Inc. Used by permission. All rights reserved.

Scripture quotations marked NLT are taken from the *Holy Bible*, New Living Translation, copyright © 1996, 2004, 2007 by Tyndale House Foundation. Used by permission of Tyndale House Publishers, Inc., Carol Stream, Illinois 60188. All rights reserved.

Scripture quotations marked NIV or NIV 84 are taken from the Holy Bible, *New International Version*,® *NIV*.® Copyright © 1973, 1978, 1984, 2011 by Biblica, Inc.™ Used by permission of Zondervan. All rights reserved worldwide. www.zondervan.com.

Scripture quotations marked *The Message* are taken from *The Message* by Eugene H. Peterson, copyright © 1993, 1994, 1995, 1996, 2000, 2001, 2002. Used by permission of NavPress Publishing Group. All rights reserved.

Scripture quotations marked AMP are taken from the *Amplified Bible*,® copyright © 1954, 1958, 1962, 1964, 1965, 1987 by The Lockman Foundation. Used by permission.

Scripture quotations marked NIrV are taken from the Holy Bible, *New International Reader's Version*,® *NIrV*.® Copyright © 1995, 1996, 1998 by Biblica, Inc.™ Used by permission of Zondervan. All rights reserved worldwide. www.zondervan.com.

Scripture quotations marked KJV are taken from the *Holy Bible*, King James Version.

Scripture quotations marked *The Voice* are taken from *The Voice New Testament*.® Copyright © 2011 by Thomas Nelson, Inc. The Voice™ translation © 2011 by Ecclesia Bible Society. Used by permission. All rights reserved.

ISBN 978-1-4143-6683-8 (sc)

Printed in the United States of America

19	18	17	16	15	14
7	6	5	4	3	

To Ken Edwards, who taught me what it means to reclaim my heart.
And to Philly Jones, who chose to fight for his
own heart and, in the end, won mine.

Contents

Acknowledgments *xi*

Excerpt from *The First Gardener* *xv*

CHAPTER 1: Heart Check *1*

CHAPTER 2: Got Heart? *27*

CHAPTER 3: Lessons from the Green *39*

CHAPTER 4: The Performing Heart *49*

CHAPTER 5: The Disappointed Heart *77*

CHAPTER 6: The Controlling Heart *101*

CHAPTER 7: The Critical Heart *119*

CHAPTER 8: The Shamed Heart *143*

CHAPTER 9: The Angry Heart *167*

CHAPTER 10: The Fearful Heart *191*

CHAPTER 11: The Weary Heart *219*

CHAPTER 12: Living with a Reclaimed Heart *241*

Notes *261*

About the Author *265*

Acknowledgments

I'M PRETTY CERTAIN few people have verses from the book of Hosea read at their wedding. But my husband Philly and I did. Our friend and counselor Ken Edwards knew us well enough to know that this passage would be especially fitting for our hearts and our stories as we started our new journey.

> Therefore, behold, I will allure her, will bring her into the wilderness, and speak comfort to her. I will give her her vineyards from there, and the Valley of Achor as a door of hope; she shall sing there, as in the days of her youth, as in the day when she came up from the land of Egypt.
> HOSEA 2:14-15

This is our story—Philly's and mine. The story of how God allured us by allowing us to walk through the wilderness of our divorces. But what it gave us was an encounter with our Savior like nothing we had ever known. It changed us. It planted new dreams in us. It gave us hope in places where dead dreams used to live. It had us both singing in our cars at the top of our lungs like those dorks you sit next to at the stoplight. It had us acting the way we did as young kids, before we allowed our hearts to be shut down.

God used the heartbreak of our pain to pull us into the heart of his love. And he did it all while bringing our own hearts back to life. This book wasn't written because we have some special story to tell. We all know heartbreak. Some of you know it because you lost your job. Some through the loss of a marriage. Some through the loss of a dream. Some through the devastating loss of a child. Wildernesses can have all different kinds of faces. But in wildernesses God longingly desires to woo us back to that childlike heart he first deposited inside us. That is the revelation we have discovered. The beautiful rediscovery of our hearts. And that is the story we felt led to share.

So to you, the reader, thank you. Thank you for trusting me with your heart on this journey. Many of you I will never have the privilege of enjoying a Coca-Cola with, but you might have Coke-stained pages. So in a small way I feel like we have met. Thank you for keeping an open heart as you read this book. You have given me your greatest treasure—and I do not take that lightly.

A special thank-you to my husband for continuing to fight the good fight for your heart and for inspiring me as I fight for mine. Very few days pass when I don't think about how grateful I am to have a life partner who loves God, loves me, and loves our family. Thank you for being willing to share your story alongside me, both in this book and in life. You are a gentle giant who makes me laugh harder than anyone else can and who loves me with a depth I didn't know was possible. What a privilege to do life with you.

A special thank-you to my friend and counselor Ken Edwards, who has been a faithful depositor to my heart. Of your wisdom and humor and belief in me. The gifts God has given you have not been lost on me. Without them this book would not exist. And I am privileged to share you with others.

A special thank-you to my editor Anne Christian Buchanan, who has a way of taking the mess that are my thoughts and bringing order to the chaos. Your gifts are extraordinary. I know this book required much of you, and you gave every ounce you had. You carried it as if it were your own, and without you it would not be the book it is. I say all the time, "It isn't just one person who writes a book." That has never been more true.

A special thank-you to my dad, who was willing to read this in advance as well. My love for the Word of God came from you. My love of teaching his Word came from you. Sorry one of your sons didn't get it. But I wouldn't trade it for the world. And thank you for reminding me that not everyone who reads this will know what an MP3 player is.

A special thank-you to Karen, Stephanie, Babette, Andrea, and the Tyndale family, who make it a privilege to do what I love.

A special thank-you to my agent, Greg Daniel. You are such a faithful man, father, husband, and a wonderful gift to work with.

And to my heavenly Father, the continual and loving Author of my story. In the days when life tried to swallow me whole and the enemy worked desperately to shut down this heart you have fought so hard for, you kept me going. I pray you give me the tenacity needed to finish the race and to keep the faith. It is a journey worth taking. And because of you, I have a heart worth fighting for. Thank you for giving me your heart when you gave me Jesus. May I steward that gift well.

"A SHUT-DOWN HEART's 'bout the saddest thing I ever see. 'Cause we all come out the womb with our hearts wide open. All sweet and trustin' and close to God. It's like we got this line runnin' straight up to heaven.

"But life can start cuttin' into that there line. Li'l cut when we li'l and sump'n sad happens or we find out somebody can do things better'n we can. More li'l cuts when we go and get married and our husband or wife does sump'n to hurt us—or maybe we don't never marry and we lonely. And it just keep comin'. When we lose sump'n or hurt somewheres or get lied on and betrayed—all that just keep sawin' at that line from heaven to that li'l alive heart. And finally it don't want to stay open no more, so it just clench up."

He held his tightened fist out in front of her, soil still clinging to it. "That be to me what a shut-down heart look like—all sad and scared and bitter, all them things. . . ."

Mackenzie shifted her boots. But still had nothing to offer.

"God okay if you mad, Miz Mackenzie. Way I figure, he hear ever'thing, so ain't much we gots to say gon' shock him. But when you take that heart he gone and placed inside you and shut it all down, well . . . don't know if there be anything make him ache more."

Mackenzie's eyebrows rose, then lowered.

. . . "Can't pretend I know where your heart be. Just know from my own 'periences that when life come at you hard, like it done come down on you now, be easy to quit livin'. And I don't want you to do that. Not when there more livin' left to do."

From Denise Hildreth Jones's *The First Gardener*, chapter 29

CHAPTER ONE

HEART CHECK

Go to your bosom; Knock there, and ask
your heart what it doth know.
WILLIAM SHAKESPEARE

I STOOD IN THE DRESSING ROOM and stared at the fancy jeans I had just put on. Then I turned around to check my rear end. I hadn't done a booty check in a pair of jeans since I don't know when. Maybe never. But at almost forty years old, recently divorced, I was doing just that.

I left the dressing room and crossed over to where my mother sat in a chair waiting for me. Then I did the "girl walk."

Most men I know have no idea what this is. When a guy tries on clothes, he does the "robotic turn"—arms slightly stuck out from his sides, he turns around in a circle as he bounces slightly from one foot to the other, looking more like a waddling pregnant lady in her ninth month. To check his rear view, he pulls at the seat of his jeans, twists his head in a contortionist manner, then shrugs and decides it's not worth the headache. They stay up. He'll buy them.

But girls or women, in my experience, do something completely different when they're in front of a dressing room mirror. A woman keeps her body facing forward, takes a step away from the three-way mirror, and turns her head slightly to see how her booty looks. Then she slowly turns around and spends the next thirty minutes doing it over and over again—as if the view will be different the last time than it was the first.

Today, every backward glance made me smile. This was a marker kind of day for me, a defining moment—almost as momentous as the decision I had made five months earlier when I chose the clothes I would wear to court to begin the process of becoming divorced.

"What do you think?" I asked my mom. This is also something girls do. They take friends to tell them how they look. Men reluctantly take their wives, if anyone.

"They look good, baby." My mom is very Southern, so these words came out slowly. The word *baby* had three syllables.

"They're not too tight?" I asked.

"No, they make your rear end look cute."

I was almost forty. *Cute* was definitely a good word.

"I travel and teach people about Jesus, Mom. Seriously, do they look too tight?"

Mom laughed. She understood. When she married my father, a young new preacher, she couldn't even wear a wedding ring because of the restrictions in the denomination he served. She was well aware of what people in ministry were often expected to wear or not wear. Plus she has always been one of the classiest, most ladylike women I know. If she approved, I could run with that.

"They look fine, baby. You know your mother wouldn't lie to you."

I flipped my head for the tenth time. If I jerked much

harder, I was going to leave with a new pair of jeans and whiplash. "They're cute, huh?"

"I like them."

"They're pricey."

"Well, I'm paying for them, so don't you worry about it." The jeans were going to be my Christmas present from my parents.

"I'm almost forty, Mom. Should I really be wearing these?"

"My forties were my best years. You enjoy wearing them."

I turned my body halfway around and studied the side shot in the mirror. The smile crept wide across my face. My fancy jeans looked really good on me. "You sure you want to get these for me?"

"Are they what you want?"

"Yeah, Mom, I really like them."

"Then let's get them."

I think I might have skipped a little as I returned to the dressing room that day. That was inappropriate, perhaps, for a woman my age but fully reflective of what was happening inside me.

You see, that moment wasn't really about jeans. Not really.

It was about something I had lost, something I was fighting desperately to regain.

My heart.

I was fighting for my open, alive, God-created heart.

Let me give you a little background to show you what I'm talking about.

When I was fifteen, I usually went to school with a pair of boxer shorts sticking out from underneath a pair of cutoff sweatpants. That was the style at the time for kids my age. My mother was tortured over my style decisions, but she never said anything. My dad did, though. "You're seriously wearing that?" he asked me a couple times when he was dropping me off at school.

"Yep. Seriously" was all I offered. My wardrobe decisions might not have pleased everyone, but they pleased me.

The next year, when we moved from Myrtle Beach to Camden, South Carolina, I decided a new school required a more mature look. I graduated from boxers and sweatpants to skirts and sweaters. I even got my own account at a little store called Clothes Tree and paid the bills with money from my part-time job at a photography studio. I developed a pretty good sense of my own style. By the end of my senior year, I was even voted "best dressed."

By this point, unfortunately, my younger brother was cutting off every T-shirt he had right smack-dab in the middle of his chest, revealing his belly button. My poor parents. Just when one of their children was getting it together, another one was losing his mind.

As a college student and later, as a young graduate, I continued to enjoy my own sense of style. I met a young man, fell in love, and eventually got married. And somewhere around that time, there was another clothing shift. I basically stopped choosing my own clothes. I let someone else—my husband—define my style. Even during our courtship, he purchased many of my clothes for me. Rarely did I buy something myself, and if I did, I sought his approval first.

Now, I'm not saying that a woman shouldn't wear clothes her husband likes. Not at all. But in my case, letting my husband pick my clothes was an outward sign of a very destructive dynamic in our marriage. I couldn't see it then, but I can see it clearly now. It had a lot to do with what was happening between us and, more importantly, what was happening inside me. Bit by bit, my heart was shutting down.

As the fractures in our marriage began to spread more quickly than the new lines forming at the edges of my eyes, I finally took a stand—over a pair of jeans he wanted me to buy. They were beautiful jeans, expensive designer jeans. But they simply weren't me.

Clothes are personal. They should be a reflection of who you are. And as pair after pair of jeans made their way to my dressing room that day, I realized none of them came close. Standing there in front of the three-way mirror, I saw what those jeans represented. The man choosing them didn't really see me. I felt I had not truly been seen in years. And I wanted to be *seen*. Not as a label, not as an image . . . just as me. As Denise.

In other words, there was no way on earth I was buying those jeans. I left the store without a single purchase.

That was a big stand for me. I was so broken back then that to take any stand at all was monumental. Those jeans represented everything wrong in my marriage, and it was the hill I chose to die on.

You know what's funny? The jeans I tried on that day, picked out for me by my former husband, were the *exact same brand* my mother bought me for Christmas the December after my divorce.

As I said, the jeans weren't really the issue. The issue was what those two moments revealed about my heart. The first spotlighted a fractured, dead heart. The second showcased an open heart coming back to life. It was another step past the one I described in my memoir, *Flying Solo*, when I chose "disposable" clothes but new shoes to go to divorce court. Now, some months later, I was giving myself permission to wear those fancy jeans. Not because anyone else on the face of the earth thought I should have them, but because my heart responded to them on that defining day, at that reclaiming moment in my story.

There is a store my second husband and I often pass whenever I can actually get him into the mall. "Babe," he will say, "whatever you do, don't buy me anything from that store." Again, he's talking about so much more than shopping. He is saying, "Let me be me. Let me be the man God created me to be." And I do—because I spent so many years *not* being the woman God created me to be.

If I say it once through our journey together, I will say it a thousand times. Once you know what it is to have your heart back, you will never let it go again. And you will do your best to never be a pawn in the enemy's scheme of shutting down someone else's heart.

How's Your Heart?

Now that I've told you a little bit about my shut-down heart and one of the many ways it revealed itself, I'd like to ask you a few questions about your own heart. This is important because understanding where we are helps us understand how to get to where we're going. (If you have the Google Maps app on your phone, it's kind of like hitting the Route button when you've taken a wrong turn.)

You see, many of us have taken wrong turns in this life we've been given, and those turns have left us feeling lost. Or angry. Or fearful. Or controlling. Or weary. Or all of the above. Closed off from the person God created us to be and heartbreakingly shut down.

Could this be you? Think about it:

- If you are no longer doing things you used to love to do or have convinced yourself they no longer mean anything to you . . .
- If you spend your time perpetually focused on the needs of others and pay no attention to your own God-designed needs and desires . . .

- ◆ If you rarely have a real belly laugh or a good cry anymore . . .
- ◆ If you rarely listen to music anymore or sing from the bottom of your toes . . .
- ◆ If you don't feel things on a deep level anymore—good feelings or bad . . .
- ◆ If you find yourself thinking often that one more car (or one more house or one more affair or one more piece of cake) will fulfill you . . .
- ◆ If you haven't cut off the television or the noise in your ears for a while and just stopped and listened to the world . . .
- ◆ If the thought of doing something spontaneous, breaking your routine, or having your plans disrupted causes your stomach to tighten . . .
- ◆ If you haven't had an honest conversation about the stuff in your life in a long time—or if you can't even imagine whom you'd have such a conversation with . . .
- ◆ If you're pretty sure that your past has disqualified you for your future . . .
- ◆ If disappointment after disappointment has left you convinced that having another dream isn't worth the pain . . .
- ◆ If it feels like other people are always pulling the strings of your life . . .
- ◆ If you haven't really tasted your food in a long time or you've forgotten what kind of clothes you like to wear . . .

. . . then it might be time for a heart check. Because laughing and loving and experiencing and feeling and tasting are all pieces of living, and some of us haven't done any of that in so long we're not sure we remember how. Some of us don't even want to try. We've been hurt, and we don't want to hurt anymore. We're tired of being let down. Or we're just plain tired. For one reason or another we've lost touch with who we really are, who God created us to be.

Friends, I understand. Believe me, I've been there. That's why I'm inviting you to take an amazing journey with me—a journey to a place of joy and freedom. What waits for you at the end of this road? Here is just a taste of the possibilities:

- You'll learn to enjoy that belly laugh, the deep-down, from-your-toes kind.
- You'll break the habit of running away from your pain and learn to run into it instead. Once you let yourself feel pain—truly feel it—you'll be able to learn from it, leave it behind, or live with it in grace instead of despair.
- You'll give yourself permission to have difficult conversations with those you love the most, and you'll be okay if there is friction or tension.
- You'll experience the freedom of releasing people to their Father instead of feeling responsible to rescue them from their pain or their anger or the consequences of their own choices.
- You'll enjoy the peace of accepting who you are and the enjoyment of just being you. That, my friend, is sweet peace.

Will all this come with a price?
Yes. A steep one.
Will it be worth everything you must do to find it?
Absolutely.

Can it really happen for you?

Without a doubt.

You see, we have all been offered an abundant life. It is our birthright as children of God, our promised gift as followers of Jesus Christ. It is what we were made for, the way we were intended to live. And yet somehow, too often, it eludes us. It's almost like it's been stolen right out from under our noses.

So often we stop at the first part of John 10:10—"The thief comes only to steal and kill and destroy." Many of us understand that part of it. We've experienced how he steals our innocence, our marriages, our loved ones, and our dreams. Yeah, we know there's a real thief out there.

But that isn't where the passage ends. There is more. Thank God there is more! The Scripture goes on to say, "I have come that they may have life, and have it to the full" (NIV). Or as the King James Version so memorably puts it, "more abundantly."

Now that is a journey so worth taking. And today, right now, as you hold this book in your hands and determine that you will turn the page, you are declaring it is a journey you need to take. An expedition to take back the abundant life that has been stolen from you. To open up what has been shut down in response to painful life experiences and less-than-stellar choices. To live as the person God created you to be, the real you Christ died to save.

My specific story may be different from yours. What I have learned about the dangers of a shut-down heart and what it takes to reclaim it came through a traumatic divorce and its aftermath. Your experience may involve a difficult childhood, a soul-destroying job, a long grind through economic hardship, or some other life circumstances. But pain is pain—and the Lord's offer of abundant life applies to any painful, shut-down circumstances in which you may find yourself.

How Do Hearts Shut Down?

I was sitting in McDonald's with my then five-year-old niece Lauren, enjoying Cokes. I was educating her on the joy of the McDonald's Coke burn and the follow-up of their salty fries when I began to study her little face. She was popping in those fries one after another. And in that moment I could see her twenty years down the road.

"Lauren, you know what?"

Her "what?" was slurred because of the four French fries she was currently chomping.

"When you grow up, you are going to be a mighty woman of God."

She never missed a beat. She just popped another French fry into her mouth and said, "I know, Aunt Niecy."

Doesn't that just take your breath away? It does mine because it is such a beautiful picture of an undamaged heart. There was no cynicism, no rolled eyes at the absurdity of my statement. There was just complete acceptance. Whether Lauren understood what I was saying or not, she was convinced of one thing: she could be anything.

You see, we don't come into this world jaded. We enter life with breathtaking dreams and open, trusting hearts, convinced that anything is possible. When we see Disney movies as little kids, we find it easy to believe that we can be Cinderella or Prince Charming, that our stories really will end with a happily ever after. We assume we can put on gold bracelets like Wonder Woman and deflect any bullets sent our way, or don a red cape and leap tall buildings in a single bound. We expect all those cakes we prepare in our Easy-Bake ovens to really be easy to bake. And we're sure that if we have just the right bat—and turn the bill of our cap just the right way—all the balls we hit will end up in the stands.

Eventually, of course, we grow up and get more realistic. And don't get me wrong—we *should* grow up. The problem comes when we grow up and forget how to *live*. When we take the hearts God designed to be alive, confident, trusting, and—most important of all—always connected to his heart, and we allow them to wither and fade.

That's not maturity. That's tragedy. And it can happen all too easily—if we don't carefully guard our hearts.

I think it's safe to say that we don't wake up one morning and say, *"This is the day I'm going to stop living. This is the day I'm going to shut down my heart."* So how does it happen? If we enter life with alive, carefree, completely abandoned hearts like my niece Lauren's, then how and why do they change?

The answer is pretty obvious: life.

Yep, life.

Life creeps in and shuts us down.

Or more accurately, we encounter difficulties in life and we shut down in response.

For some of us, this happened in our childhood. Maybe it came in the form of stolen innocence—sexual abuse—or the trauma of physical or verbal abuse.

I remember a time when Tyler Perry, the creator of my favorite movie character, Madea, and the writer of my favorite movie, *Diary of a Mad Black Woman,* appeared on *Oprah* and talked about the sexual abuse he endured as a child. Oprah showed two pictures of him—one taken before the abuse and one taken afterward. He said, in essence, that the second picture, the one with "sad eyes," marked the place where his young heart shut down.

But it's not just abuse that can shut down a child's heart. For some of us, death, divorce, family illness, or other circumstances caused adult responsibilities to fall on small shoulders that were never meant to carry them. Those years that were supposed to be lived out in wonder and delight succumbed prematurely to the demands of an adult world. Instead of maturing in a healthy way and becoming healthy adults, we shut down in our childhood.

For some of us, a rigid family code motivated us to shut down. Whether overt or implied, the message we internalized was "In our family, we are to look like _____, act like _____, be like _____." (I'll let you fill in your own blanks.) Instead of being allowed to live out of our individual, God-designed hearts, we were given a box to squeeze ourselves into. Over time, we were molded into the person our family code required us to be, and the person God created us to be got lost in the shuffle.

For others of us, school was the place where our hearts began to shut down. Maybe the other kids picked on us or bullied us or branded us with an identity that haunted us year after year. (Bullying for even minor things like hair color or a lisp can leave lingering scars.) Maybe we moved a lot and grew weary of starting over. Or maybe a learning disability made school such a struggle that we finally gave up, convinced we were just dumb.

Even if we made it through high school unscathed, college might have brought us up short. Gone were the days when everybody knew our name. We were lucky if anyone recognized us at all. Some of us felt rejection for the first time. We didn't get into the sorority. We weren't the best player on the football team anymore. We didn't make the grades we thought we'd make. Insecurity and that seed of rejection settled in our souls, and we shut down our hearts to protect them.

Or maybe college birthed another dynamic: it caused us to push harder. We had to be the best student, the best athlete, or the best sorority member. Our real hearts got lost in the land of expectations—the ones we placed on ourselves as well as the ones others placed on us.

For still others of us, it happened after we graduated college. Other kids had graduated college too, and that dream job we thought would be ours just never showed up. Instead, we found ourselves working in jobs we hated alongside people who didn't value us, doing work that was less than inspiring.

Or maybe it happened after we got married. Prince Charming didn't turn out to be quite so charming. In fact, he was pretty messed up. And Cinderella came with issues—lots of them.

Truth be told, a lot of our "stuff" doesn't make its appearance until we get married. Intimacy does that. It brings out what is on the inside. And inside that covenantal place, the wounds from our past can roar to life. The residue from childhood abuse can cause us to despise our spouse's touch. The emotional fallout from having parents divorce can make us distrustful, manipulative, or detached from relationships. And in the midst of that crucible, both partners can end up thinking it would be easier simply to exist than to dig in and heal.

For still others, it happened when Prince Charming or Cinderella never showed up. We waited and waited, with no sign of a fairy-tale romance—or any romance at all. The years ticked by until the ticking clock became a banging gong. And with each dateless Valentine's Day, each ridiculous bridesmaid's dress, each bachelor party that we're expected to be the life of, our hearts shut down a little more.

And the process didn't stop there. In fact, life still comes at us as certainly as waves to the seashore. It comes with health issues and financial issues and children issues and parent issues and career and church issues. With each crashing wave, instead of falling at the feet of our Creator, many of us just fall deeper and deeper into the lie that life will never be any more than what it is. The cumulative effect leaves us asking, "If this is life, why should I even show up at all?"

And that's when it happens. That's when we hide out, go numb, give up. We close off our hearts layer by layer, piece by piece. John Eldredge describes it like this: "After a while, the accumulation of event after event that we do not like and do not understand erodes our confidence that we are part of something grand and good, and reduces us to a survivalist mind-set."[1] But even as we cling to survival, something may be dying.

Yes, I said *dying* because what happens to our hearts really is a matter of life and death. We're not just talking about jeans here—or whatever the symptoms of your shut-down heart may be. We're talking about what is taking place in the deepest part of us. If we don't wake up to the condition of our hearts and make a commitment to reclaim what has been lost and strengthen what remains, then death really will be the result.

I don't think I could put it more plainly. A completely shut-down heart is a dead heart. And because our hearts are where we link to God, the consequences can be eternal.

Journey of a Shut-Down Heart

If I could turn back time in my life, I would want someone to sit me down and share with me the stories and ideas I'm going to share with you. I wish someone had looked at me fifteen years ago and said, "More than anything you do, Denise, grab your heart and don't let go. Fight for it more than you fight for anything else."

But nobody told me that—or if they did, I couldn't hear them. I had to walk through the most difficult places, get to the end of myself, and experience what it's like to live with a shut-down heart. Then I had to fight with everything I had to get my heart opened again. Here's how it happened with me.

I grew up with parents who assured me I could be anything. They gave me and my brothers every opportunity to pursue our gifts and desires, including lessons in piano, voice, acting, and tennis. There was nothing we desired that they didn't do their best to make available to us, even with their limited resources. And what I desired most of all was to be a singer.

My father was a pastor, so I always had unfettered access to our church's sound system, and I made full use of it. I would often be late to school because I was at the church singing. As soon as I got home from school, I'd head straight to the church and sing. On weekends, singing was the first thing I wanted to do. As soon as church was over on Sunday and we had cleaned up after dinner, I would go sing.

All through my middle school and high school years, singing was my passion. But I had no idea whether I could ever make a living with my music, so I developed a backup plan. I majored in broadcast journalism at the University of South Carolina, though I took private voice lessons all through college and continued to look for opportunities to break into the music industry.

At one point I thought beauty pageants might afford me the opportunity I was seeking. So I entered the Miss South Carolina pageant—twice!—with hopes that the Miss America stage would open a door for me to become a professional musician. I won the talent competition once and became a finalist both times but still came up short of the crown. Some painful circumstances that unfolded during the competition convinced me that Miss America wasn't the vehicle to get me to my dreams.

When college was over, I had some decisions to make. I began to ask the Lord what he had for me, and it soon became clear that I was not to stay in my hometown in South Carolina. Nashville—or Music City, as some have named it—seemed the ideal place for a girl who dreamed of being a singer. So I took all my college graduation money and moved to Tennessee. (I'm sure there is a sad country song in here somewhere.) A cousin who was a Christian recording artist offered me a place to stay. I took care of his children while he and his wife were on the road. Meanwhile, I was looking for a real job and working on a demo CD to send to record labels.

After three months of living with family, I was finally able to move out on my own. I got a job as a receptionist in the parts department of a heating and air-conditioning company, working with a woman who cussed like a sailor, chain-smoked, and wore mink coats on the job. I adored her, but being a receptionist in the parts department wasn't what I had envisioned for my life. I still dreamed of singing professionally, but as the rejections started coming in from my demo, I began to suspect that God might have different plans for me, at least in the short term.

Fortunately I still had an outlet for my passion. I had found an amazing church in Nashville whose choir had received numerous music awards. It was one of the elite choirs in the Christian music industry, and I became part of it. While at this church, I met the man I would marry. And it was somewhere around then that things started to go wrong with my heart.

You see, the level of talent in the choir was unbelievable. It included backup singers for some of the most famous artists in country and Christian music. As I encountered more and more gifted singers, insecurities I never even knew I had began to surface. To make matters worse, my future husband was part of a legendary recording group. He had a voice few could rival—especially mine. I had been pretty good in the small pond where

I grew up. But this was the ocean I had been thrown into, and he was a really big fish.

Though I loved being around him, I felt the distinction acutely. The more time we spent together, the more my own dream of being a singer dwindled. Amid all the wonderful music, my own voice grew faint.

I didn't know it at the time, but a piece of my heart was shutting down.

We married a month shy of my twenty-fifth birthday, and the shutting-down process accelerated from there. Very early in our marriage, I knew something was seriously wrong in our relationship. I reached out to some people I trusted and shared with them my concerns, but they didn't seem able to help. I was young, and I had been raised to believe marriage was forever. So I did the best I knew to do. Unfortunately that involved handing over piece after piece of my true self.

I gave up my opinions to keep the peace. I fudged my convictions to avoid arguments. I second-guessed my instincts and pushed down certain aspects of my personality and, yes, even my taste in clothes. And I surrendered most of my dreams, including my lifelong dream of being a mother, because it seemed the life I was living left me no choice. Piece by piece the vibrant, alive woman God had created me to be all but disappeared.

If you had asked me at the time what was going on with me, I might have said I was making sacrifices out of love. I might have said something about the importance of compromise. I might have told you I was fighting for my marriage. In many ways I was. And I still believe those things are both necessary and important. I often tell people that the Bible clearly says God hates divorce and anyone who has been divorced knows why.

But what I was doing in those days was less about sacrifice

and compromise and more about hiding from the truth of our relationship. I was avoiding pain, running from confrontation. In a sense, I was treating my marriage as an idol—sacrificing my dearest possession, my truest self, to a false god.

I had always assumed that people who got divorced just hadn't worked on their marriages hard enough, and I was pretty sure I'd be judged that way if I got divorced. So I was absolutely determined to give my marriage everything I had, no matter what it took. But in my arrogance, in my deepest places of disillusionment and pride, and in my twisted ways of thinking, I was really handing over my heart to the thief who came to destroy.

And I was definitely paying the price. I looked ten years older than I look today—as my friends will tell you and pictures will reveal. I was tired and worn and all but dead inside. Large groups intimidated me. I'd sit like a wallflower. I lived those years inside of my marriage telling people, "My college years were the best years of my life." Every time those words flew out of my mouth, I would wonder what people thought of me. But I couldn't help it. It was true.

A Gentle Wooing

And yet, do you know what God was doing during those years? He was gently inviting me to encounter him, to discover what he had for me. And he did it in that sweet way of his—by graciously offering me opportunities to connect to my heart and remind me of who I really was. But it wasn't until after my divorce, after I had begun to reclaim my heart, that I actually realized what he had been doing.

Six years into my marriage, for instance, when I was in an extremely broken place, God gave me the idea of a crazy character named Savannah. She was so compelling to me that I wrote a series of novels about her. Savannah said anything she wanted to say, did anything she wanted to do. She was a bit of a mess at times, but she was also completely alive.

When I handed the first Savannah book to an agent friend of mine and asked her to read it, she came back to me with these words. "Denise, I bet this is what you're really like somewhere deep down in there."

I believe her words were God's words to me—as direct a message as any he has ever spoken to my heart. Because Savannah was me—or at least the me I had been. Looking back now, I can see that God was giving me a chance to try to grab my heart back. Sadly, I didn't understand that at the time. All I knew was that for a couple hours a day, when I sat down in front of my computer and wrote about this vibrant, alive young woman, my heart was alive too. It would be a while before I realized that same heart was available to me every day.

My counselor, Ken Edwards, told me years later, "God will woo us to him or push us to him." That is so true. Looking back, I can see that God was wooing me through Savannah. Not forcing, not pushing yet, but gently calling me back to himself. He also wooed me through opportunities to teach his Word in Bible studies and seminars. I have been privileged for the past fifteen years to minister across this nation and overseas. Each time I teach, my heart is connected to that deep, authentic place of my Father. And even through that "dead" season of my life, God gave me those breathless moments of delivering his Word. For a brief time I would know what it was to be my true, best, most alive self. Then I would return home to my shut-down cocoon.

I'm not one of those people who lives with no regrets. Yes, I know all the decisions I have made brought me to the place I am today, and I am very grateful for this place. But I do have regrets. Countless regrets. Things I wish I could do over, do differently. Words I wish had never come out of my mouth. Choices I wish I had never made. One of the many regrets of my first marriage is that I missed God's wooing in those days. Because even with the respite of my writing and my teaching, it wasn't until I reached the pushing place and the pain of my divorce that I started getting serious about reclaiming my heart.

I have often wondered what would have happened had I dared to begin to reclaim my heart inside of my marriage. I will never know. It might have made a difference, or the marriage might simply have ended sooner. What I do know is the first day I sat on my counselor's sofa to begin to unravel the mess that was my life, I said, "Whatever got me here, I want it out of me." I see now that I was really saying, "I want to live. Really live. I want my heart back." But it took me a while to get there.

You have to understand how shut down I was by that time. I didn't even know what I liked. As I've mentioned, my husband bought virtually all my clothes—jeans included. I had worn my hair pretty much the same way for years, in a short bob, because that's the way it was when he met me and that was how he liked it. He was a gifted interior designer, so he chose our furniture and decorated our home. He always asked me what I liked, but I almost always said, "Whatever you pick is fine with me."

And let me make this clear: my husband wasn't *doing* all this to me.

I was doing it to me.

Because the truth is, no one can shut down another person's heart.

Did you get that? I'm going to repeat it, and I want you to read it slowly and then underline or highlight it: *No one has the power to shut down another person's heart.* Handing over our hearts is always a choice, just as handing over our peace or our joy is a choice.

That's not to say it's always a conscious or deliberate choice. In extreme cases, such as severe abuse, it may be an automatic response, a God-given self-protective mechanism. And even in my case, I didn't plan to shut down my heart. I simply responded to circumstances the best way I knew, day after day, using tools that felt natural to me but turned out to be counterproductive. But those were still choices on my part, even if their end result was to cut me off from the life I was meant to have.

My husband did not shut down my heart, in other words. I chose to hand it over. That was my sin—because, as we will discover in our journey together, shutting down our hearts is always sin. And to resurrect my heart, I had to *choose* to recognize my sin, own it, and repent of it.

I say all that to make it clear that I am in no way blaming my former husband for the state of my heart. I'm just thankful that somewhere in the course of running headlong into the intense pain of my divorce—and running headlong into the heart of my Father—I finally made the choice to change direction.

Opening Up

So what has this change of direction been like? For me, it's been a gradual but deliberate process of rediscovering my authentic feelings and my personal tastes, daring to confront the misconceptions and misguided decisions that kept me shut down. Some of these might seem trivial, but for me they were pivotal in my journey to open my shut-down heart.

The jeans are definitely a case in point. But let me give you a few more examples.

One day several months after my divorce, Ken encouraged me to go to the bookstore and buy five magazines that were not what I usually purchased. "Just let your eyes scan the magazines and see what your *heart* gravitates toward."

I was shocked—completely shocked—to discover that my heart gravitated to home magazines. Four of the five I bought were about decorating. I had never hung a picture! My mother had always decorated our homes, and she and my godmother had even decorated my first apartment. Then I married, and my husband did the decorating. Learning I had the slightest hint of interest in a fabric swatch or paint color was a revelation to me.

When I remarried and moved into my new husband's house, he said, "Make this your home, babe." And I did. For one solid week I did nothing but design our home. I hung every picture. Placed every piece of furniture and every accessory. Covered my piano with family photographs the way I had always wanted to do. I don't know that I have ever enjoyed a week the way I enjoyed that one.

I also didn't cut my hair for anything other than a trim for a year following my divorce. I discovered I love it long. I've highlighted it and wear it wavy and curly and wild. I've had fun exploring my personal fashion sense too. It is sometimes classic, sometimes trendy, and totally me. I've found that I am good at all of it—at styling my clothes and styling my hair and styling my home. More than that, I feel alive when I'm doing those things.

One of the greatest joys of my reclaimed heart is bringing music back into my life. By the time of my divorce, I hadn't bought a CD for years. Oh, I sang along during worship at church but never spontaneously. The girl who used to be late to class because she was so caught up in singing had closed music so far off from her soul that she didn't even tune in to music stations in the car. It was talk radio all the time.

But when I began to reclaim my heart, I reclaimed my love

for music as well. I spent hundreds of dollars on music downloads, and I started singing again—loud and often! As the music took its rightful place in my life, my heart opened wider and wider.

And then, somewhere along my journey to reclaim my heart, something really wonderful happened. I met and fell in love with a man who was on the same journey from shut down to open and alive. Eventually we married. Our life together has been a revelation to me—not perfect, but real and satisfying.

If a fear haunts me, it is this: that I would ever allow my heart to return to its lost, barren, shut-down state. And that's always a possibility, especially when I face challenging situations.

For instance, when I married Philly, he came with his own broken places—places he has fought hard to reclaim and continues to fight for—and there have been times when my brokenness rubs up against his.

Marrying Philly also meant I took on the role of "bonus mom" to his five amazing children—four girls and a boy, who at the time of our marriage were thirteen, twelve, eleven, nine, and seven. This new family was truly an answer to prayer, something I wasn't sure would ever happen. But the truth is, it's not easy to build a relationship with five kids who still struggle with their parents' divorce, who can't help but see my presence as a perpetual reminder that their mom and dad will never get back together. The challenges we face as a blended family sometimes make me want to run and hide—and I mean that literally as well as figuratively. We had a running joke for our first couple years of marriage: "If you want to find Denise, she's probably in her closet." And I was. It was the only place in my house that felt safe to me.

So there are still times in our life together when I let my fears control me, causing me not to be genuinely Denise. There are still days when my insecurities remove me from being fully present in our lives.

But now I fight it! I fight hard to keep my heart alive because I know what it's like to be shut down. And I have decided I will never live there again. Never.

My Challenge to You

I don't want you to live there either—no matter what circumstances have influenced you to shut down your heart.

You might be like I was—so shut down you don't know who you are anymore. Maybe you haven't bought your own clothes in years, or maybe the only time you actually voice your opinion is at drive-through windows when no one else is in the car telling you what you should order. Or maybe you're not quite that shut down, but something in my description still feels a little too close to home. Or you might even have a huge desire to toss this book back up on a shelf or return it to the friend who gave it to you. Maybe you are still in a place of thinking everything that has happened to you is someone else's fault. Maybe you're simply not ready to reclaim your heart, and that's okay.

But if any of what I've said sounds the least bit familiar, I hope you'll consider that God might be wooing you. Maybe he's inviting you, in the safety of your own home or during your lunch break at the office or on a beach chair listening to the music that only God can make, to take a journey that might actually change the very course of your life.

Let me assure you of one thing: when the Creator of the universe took the extreme care that he did in fashioning you, he made you unique and precious, and he gave you the power of choice. Nothing that has happened to you since then—not even the pain of abuse, betrayal, or failure—can take away that power from you. If events beyond your control have caused you to shut down without giving it a thought, you *still* have a choice of what you will do with your future.

No one can take your God-designed, alive heart away from you. Only you can hand it over. And only you—with God's gracious help—can take it back.

There may be moments on this journey when you need to take a breather. I understand that. There may be moments when you need to put down the book and have a meltdown. Lord knows I've had those too. There may even be moments when you need to stop reading entirely and encounter all the pain you have run from for years.

But I can assure you of this. The first time you hear yourself belly laugh again . . . the first time your spouse touches you and something inside you tingles . . . the first time the laughter of a child awakens you to something deep in the soul of you . . . the first time you sing in the car again like you're Celine Dion or Harry Connick Jr. . . . . the first time you buy your own clothes or pick out your own dinner or decide how you want to wear your hair or state your opinion out loud . . . you will be grateful that you were brave enough to keep reading.

Yes, I said it, *brave enough*—because reclaiming your heart takes courage. It takes work too—the work of honestly examining your life and then being intentional with different choices. But it's so worth it. With God's help, you can reclaim your shut-down heart and run headlong into your amazing future.

Let me assure you. From the other side . . . the view is breathtaking.

CHAPTER TWO

GOT HEART?

When your heart speaks, take good notes.
JUDITH CAMPBELL

THE QUESTION WAS A TEST, just like so many they had asked Jesus. In fact, they loved testing him. A lawyer was the one asking: "Teacher, which is the most important commandment in the law of Moses?" (Matthew 22:36, NLT).

Jesus had an immediate response. He didn't always. Sometimes he paused and wrote in the sand. But this time the reply was quick. He answered with something God had told the children of Israel centuries before: "You must love the LORD your God with all your heart, all your soul, and all your mind" (v. 37, referencing Deuteronomy 6:5, NLT).

Like Father, like Son—the biggest answers to the biggest questions have been and always will be about the heart. As God told Samuel when he anointed David as king, "The LORD doesn't see things the way you see them. People judge by outward appearance, but the LORD looks at the heart" (1 Samuel 16:7, NLT).

But what does *heart* really mean in the Scripture and in our lives? We've already talked a lot about hearts in this book—shutting them down, handing them over, reclaiming them, letting them come back to life. It should be obvious that we're not talking about the physical muscle that pumps blood through the body. But beyond that, *heart* means different things to different people. To some it refers to emotion as opposed to intellect—as in, "Rely on your head and not your heart." Others think of it strictly in terms of romantic love—as in almost every pop song ever written.

But in this book I am referring to something much deeper and more important. I'm speaking of *heart* as the Bible often refers to it—as the absolute center of the self, that part of us that is most intrinsically us. It is the place in us where our feelings and reactions and purposes are most authentic, the place where we are most truly alive. Our deepest, truest longings and desires come from our hearts. So do our thoughts and our wills. True personality is rooted there. Deep understanding and intuition originate there as well.

Most importantly, our hearts are where we connect with God.

If you're the analytical type, this might raise a few questions, especially when you think of Jesus' response to the lawyer. His answer is absolutely key in this book, but it does raise another question. Jesus said we are to love God with all our hearts and souls and minds. (The gospels of Mark and Luke add the word *strength*.) So was Jesus implying that *heart* and *soul* and *mind* are different things?

Some people think so, and they spin complex—and sometimes contradictory—descriptions of which part does what.

They have a lot to say about the distinctions between *spirit* and *soul* too, as well as the philosophical and linguistic implications of these terms in the Hebrew and the Greek.[1]

It's all interesting and worth some study. But to be honest, I'm not interested in being quite that technical. As I read it, the Bible itself doesn't do that. Jesus didn't go into an exegetical study with the lawyer that day. Instead, the distinctions he seemed to make were far more fluid. And throughout the Bible, terms like *heart* and *soul* and *mind* (not to mention *spirit* and *strength*) are often used interchangeably. So while I don't claim to have the final word on any of this, I'm leery about being too rigid with these distinctions.

For the purposes of our journey together, when I talk about the heart, I'm simply referring to "the essential or most vital part" of who we are.[2] It's the center of our souls and the focus of our true identities, the part of us that we are to guard "above all else."

Did you catch that? The Bible tells us, "Above all else, guard your heart" (Proverbs 4:23, NIV). Of all the aspects of our life we should value and protect—our possessions, our health, our families, our time—our hearts must get top priority.

But why? Why is guarding the heart so important?

The answer is found in the second part of this verse: ". . . for everything you do flows from it." In other words, it affects everything you do. We're to guard our hearts because what happens in our hearts—that central, essential part of us—impacts everything else that happens in our lives.

So if everything we do, in every area of our lives, depends on our hearts, it's easy to understand why guarding them is of such vital importance. Because if a heart isn't guarded, if it becomes closed, shut down, boarded up, disconnected from everyday life, then every aspect of life—dreams, callings, relationships—will be affected.

If we're married, our sex life may suffer. If we're parents, we may give our children nothing of value except the bare minimum to get through the day. Some of us may do just enough work to not lose our jobs—or give up working entirely. Still others may simply fake their way through life. We may speak up at the ladies' Bible study, run the deacons' meeting, maybe even "do our duty" in the bedroom, but we will offer little of true worth.

An alive heart, an open heart, is a "wellspring of life," as an older version of the NIV (1984) puts it. A *wellspring* is defined as "a source of continual supply."[3] That is what an alive heart does; it brings a continual supply of life to every pursuit. A shutdown heart is cut off at the source and can provide no life at all.

The heart, in other words, is the key to everything else. Not a bank account. Not social status. Not the way we look (though our culture tries hard to convince us otherwise). The wellspring of life is and always has been the heart.

I remember watching *Survivor* a while back with my husband and my oldest daughter. There was this gorgeous girl on the show. I mean *gorgeous*—smooth tan skin, glossy dark hair, and a knockout figure in a yellow bathing suit. But she was also sneaky and conniving. My husband looked at me one night while we were watching and said, "Can you imagine being married to her?" His remark reminded me that though any heart can recognize natural beauty, an alive heart gravitates to *true* beauty. From-the-heart beauty. In the long run, no amount of Botox or Hydroxycut or even natural, unadulterated Jennifer Lopez or Brad Pitt good looks or power can compensate for a heart that is shut down.

From the Heart

The Jews in Jesus' day were obsessed with rules. They liked things to be cut-and-dried, black-and-white, right or wrong.

That's why the lawyer asked Jesus what the greatest commandment was. He wanted to pin him down about what rules people most needed to follow in order to be right with God.

Of course, Jesus turned the question on its ear—by summing up all the laws with a simple (but not easy!) call to loving relationships. The lawyer wanted to talk about rules, but Jesus insisted on talking about relationships. About the heart.

A man named Saul was obsessed with rules too—until he had an encounter with the real God of the universe on the road to Damascus. That encounter changed his heart. It even changed his name. The man formerly known as Saul, the hater of Gentiles, became Paul, the man who would be the catalyst in reaching them with the gospel of Jesus Christ.

But in addition to reaching the Gentiles, Paul also wanted to speak to people just like himself—good people who had fallen for the dangerous lie that relationship with God depends on following rules and acting rightly. What happened on the Damascus road convinced him that a connection with the Almighty (and anyone else) is most of all about the heart. That's why Paul stressed, "If you confess with your mouth the Lord Jesus and *believe in your heart* that God has raised Him from the dead, you will be saved" (Romans 10:9, emphasis added).

This was a completely new way of thinking for them, and it's still a foreign way of thinking for many of us. But it's a fundamental and transforming truth—that our very lives depend on engaging our hearts.

Engaging the heart is what brings us into relationship with God. Intimacy grows when we love him passionately, trust him completely, and put him first in our lives. And in that intimacy, following his rules becomes our desire, not his demand.

Engaging the heart is also what brings us into relationship with others. It's what affords us the sweet fellowship of communion over meals with friends, true intimacy with a spouse, or life-giving conversations with our children.

And our very salvation comes by engaging and opening our hearts to the truth that Jesus is real. That he died. That he was buried and rose again. In this sense, too, the heart is the wellspring of life. It's the conduit by which we receive eternal life.

Now I'm not talking about some flannelgraphs from your vacation Bible school days or some myth we have discounted. I am talking about the God of the universe who designed our hearts in the first place, who created us for relationships and desires a relationship with us. Where? Yes. In our hearts.

A few years ago, when I finally began teaching again following my divorce, I asked God to send in people who had never been saved. I didn't want to just grow a Bible study. I wanted to reach the lost. And there, on the very first day of the study, was a woman named Helen.[4]

Helen's first husband had left her and she became a single mother at a young age. In her thirties she met a man who fell in love with her and wanted to adopt her children. He went to a nearby church, and though Helen wasn't a believer, she agreed to take her kids and try it out.

The pastor's message that day happened to be about divorce, and the judgments and opinions he offered from the pulpit lacerated Helen's already-wounded heart. Helen vowed never to go to church again and, for many years, didn't. She wanted nothing to do with the God she'd heard about there. Even years later when her daughter, now grown, attended one of my Bible studies and tried to get her mother to come, Helen refused.

I don't know why Helen changed her mind this time, but I'm glad she did. I opened the very first lesson by sharing about my own divorce, the shame and pain it involved, and what a redeeming and loving Father we have. And as Helen later told me, something happened to her that morning. "All of a sudden, I just knew in my heart that all of those things I had heard about Jesus were true."

Where did that change happen? In Helen's heart—because the heart is where all relationships begin, especially a relationship with God. That's why God cares so much about the state of our hearts. Why Jesus said the greatest commandment is to "love the LORD your God with all your heart (and soul and mind and strength)." Why Paul wanted people from every nation to realize that believing in Jesus with their hearts was the only thing that would save them.

Satan's Favorite Target

Now, if our hearts are this vital—vital to salvation, vital to an intimate love relationship with our heavenly Father and with the people God has put into our lives—then it should be blatantly evident that the enemy of our souls is after them. Ferociously. Remember, "the thief comes . . . to steal and kill and destroy." We could safely say, "The thief comes to steal our hearts, kill our hearts, shut down our hearts, and destroy our hearts . . ." along with our marriages, our children, our hopes, our dreams.

Want me to go on? The list never stops. But if the enemy can get our hearts, if he can reach in there and grab hold of the very center of our beings, the place where relationship with God resides, where the truth of who Jesus is and what he can be to us is known, then Satan doesn't have to work for the other stuff. That will follow. Because each of those things can easily be lost when we stop guarding our hearts and allow them to shut down.

How exactly does the enemy go about shutting down our hearts? He has many tactics, but his favorite weapon is lying about God. He gets to our hearts by slanderous accusations about the One who made us and loves us and longs for face-to-face encounters with us. The enemy is ruthless in his effort to get us to believe something that is untrue about the heart of our heavenly Father. Because if he can do that, he can put a wedge between us and our Creator, then shut us down with worry or fear or anger or shame.

And we fall for it all the time! Every shut-down heart is based on one or more of these lies about our God. I certainly fell for several of them in my own journey. I've always treasured and loved God's Word. I have been a student of the Word and lived in it for mere survival in the most difficult seasons of my life. I have led Bible studies for years. I've even spoken for the Billy Graham Evangelical Association. But when I let down the guard of my heart, when I offered it up to the lesser gods of my fear and my anger and my shame, I learned how easy it is for any of us, even Bible teachers and authors, to succumb to the lies of the enemy.

Life, Death, and Sin

The enemy is relentless. He is a master at deception. He is a liar. He will do everything he can to get us to let down our guard, believe his slander, and fall into sin.

Make no mistake: Shutting down your heart is indeed a sin.

Let me say that again: Shutting down your heart is a sin.

I can't make it sound any prettier than it is, nor will I try. Because when we stop guarding our hearts and allow them to shut down, we are disobeying God, and that's sin. In many cases, we end up handing our hearts over to someone or something else and giving that person or thing a godlike role in our lives, which is idolatry—also a sin. Believing the enemy's lies—especially his lies about God—is most definitely a sin. And the Bible tells us quite plainly that "the wages of sin is death" (Romans 6:23, NLT).

I'm not saying shutting down is an automatic death sentence. That's the whole point of the gospel, isn't it? After all, there's more to Romans 6:23: "For the wages of sin is death, but the free gift of God is eternal life through Christ Jesus our Lord" (NLT).

The Bible makes it clear that there is a remedy to sin, that heart death isn't inevitable. We don't have to live like dead men walking. But we can't take advantage of the remedy God offers unless we're willing to recognize the sin in the first place and to repent, to change direction. And it is important to remember that with sin something always dies.

May I give you a picture of just how seriously God takes this? Look at the words directed to the church of Sardis in Revelation 3:1-3:

> I know all the things you do, and that you have a reputation for being alive—but you are dead. Wake up! Strengthen what little remains, for even what is left is almost dead. I find that your actions do not meet the requirements of my God. Go back to what you heard and believed at first; hold to it firmly. Repent and turn to me again. If you don't wake up, I will come to you suddenly, as unexpected as a thief (NLT).

The words are not sugarcoated here. God isn't fooled by externals. We may look good on Sunday mornings in our church pew or on Monday mornings when we walk into the office. Our friends may think we have it all together. We may have the nice suit, the pretty dress, the right address, but God truly knows what's really going on in our lives. He knows every tear we cry. He knows the fists that beat the steering wheel or punch holes in the wall. He knows the brokenness inside us. He knows that even *feeling* anger would be a relief for some and *not* feeling anger would be a relief for others.

"I know where you live," he is saying. If your heart is even beginning to shut down, he doesn't want you to stay there. "Pay attention," he urges. "Repent. Wake up. Strengthen what remains. Pay attention to the state of your heart while there's still time."

Why is he so adamant about all this? Because our hearts are precious to him. Everything we do flows from them, remember? They are the wellspring of life. It doesn't get more valuable than that.

That is why it is so important to stop the blame game here. Your mama isn't reading this book. Your daddy isn't reading this book. Your husband or wife isn't reading this book. The person who hurt you all those years ago isn't reading this book. *You* are reading this book. And you are the only one who can make the choice to reclaim your heart.

Imagine you're sitting in the doctor's office right now, reading this book because you know you'll be waiting at least two hours before a nurse even thinks about calling your name. (This is why you should always have something interesting to read when you go to the doctor's office.) Then you finally get some face time with the doctor, and he shakes his head. "Well," he tells you, "unless you make some major changes in your life, you'll be dead within the year."

That would be a wake-up call, wouldn't it? I can guarantee you'd do a lot of things differently in your life after you heard the doctor's words.

So the God who says, "I have come that they may have life" is saying right now—no, I think he is shouting—"Wake up . . . before it's too late!"

Grace for Your Journey

"Denise, you have no idea what I've been through."

You're right. And I'm so sorry for what you've been through.

"Denise, I've been this way a long time. I don't even know where to begin."

Beginning is the hardest part.

"Denise, I want to know what it is to live again."

Oh, my friend, I want you to know that too. Your heavenly Father does as well. I believe that is why he has allowed this truth to come into your life at this moment.

I've said before it won't be easy. I know. I've done it. I continue to do it.

But what I also know is that there is an immeasurable grace for your journey—grace far deeper and wider and higher than what we can come up with on our own.

I once heard T. D. Jakes describe what happens when his children bring their own children—his grandkids—over to his house. It was something like "God gave me the grace I needed to raise you, but I don't have that grace anymore." In other words: "Don't even think about leaving these kids here too long."

That made me think of the time Philly took our five kids and their friends to Six Flags, back when the smallest one was still in a stroller. Nine kids. One man. Six Flags. He needed monumental amounts of grace just to survive.

I also remember telling my mother years ago, when I was trying to figure out what to do with my broken marriage, "I just don't want to live my life being labeled as a divorced woman."

She said, "Baby, if you ever get there, God will be waiting with the grace you need."

I did. And he was. And I learned a powerful lesson about grace, which is that God gives us all the grace we need for the individual seasons—and even moments—of our lives. When we need it, it's there for us.

We can't determine how we'll act or behave in situations

we've never been in before. Why? Because God's grace is in this moment. This season. And he has the grace you need for this journey.

- The grace to wake up and strengthen what remains.
- The grace to begin to change those old entrenched, habitual patterns of behavior.
- The grace to move from automatic responses triggered by pain in our past or present to more intentional and healthy ones.
- The grace to recognize that it is time to change.
- The grace to know it won't happen all at once but will be a journey. A process.
- The grace to do the hard work and the self-examination a journey like this requires.

My friend, every bit of the grace you need is available to you. God wants your heart to be open and alive even more than you do. He is the Source of all life in the first place. And he knows you better than anyone, even yourself.

You can trust him with your heart. He is wooing you now— right now, as you read this book. If you keep turning to him instead of hiding, choosing at every juncture to ask for his strength and protection, remembering that the point is to love with all your heart and soul and mind and strength, you won't stay shut down for long. In fact, if we ever get the opportunity to sit down over a McDonald's Coke and some fries and I look at you and say, "Do you know what a mighty woman (or man) of God you are?" you won't miss a beat.

You'll simply pop in another fry and say, "I know, Denise. I know." And you'll be what you were always meant to be— a mighty woman or man of God.

CHAPTER THREE

LESSONS FROM THE GREEN

As you walk down the fairway of life you must smell
the roses, for you only get to play one round.
BEN HOGAN

MY HUSBAND LOVES GOLF. And he's good at it—so good that
I bought him a round of golf at Pebble Beach Golf Links for a
Valentine's, anniversary, Christmas, and birthday gift. Yep, that
gift was good enough to represent a year's worth of celebra-
tion. That beautiful California golf course is a mecca for serious
golfers. It's even hosted the US Open multiple times.

The day Philly used his gift, he played with a couple from
South Africa who were doing a tour of the best golf courses
in the world. After their round of golf with my husband, they
were headed to New York, then Australia and China. The
other young man in the foursome was from Charlotte, North
Carolina. He had just lost his mother to cancer and was using
this trip as a time to heal. He had played the course four days
in a row.

What impressed me about the Pebble Beach course as I walked many of the holes with my husband were the breathtaking views it offered. I can't even describe them, and the pictures I took don't do them justice. You have to be there to fully grasp the beauty and magic the course holds. And being there was the deciding factor in my decision to take up golf.

I had other reasons, of course. For one thing, I'm getting older, and I'll need activity as the years go by that doesn't require strenuous cycling or running (both of which I hate). Another reason is that Philly loves the sport, and doing it with him will keep us talking. The chance to be outdoors on those beautiful courses was also certainly a factor. But most importantly, I have always been sports challenged. (Case in point: I played on a church softball team when I was in college until my cousin finally let me know they might be better off without me.) Golf seemed to be one I could handle. Club. Ball. Cart. Nature. Me against myself. This, I thought, I could do.

But all that aside, and all sarcasm aside, golf was something I wanted to do just for me, a gift to my own heart. Something that would have nothing to do with ministry, studying, writing, paying bills, doing laundry, or grocery shopping. It wasn't about someone else's needs or wants. I have long struggled with granting myself permission to do things for myself. But I was finally ready, and golf seemed the perfect choice.

I signed up for a ladies' clinic at the beautiful par-three course in Franklin, Tennessee, where we live. But no one except me, apparently, was willing to brave the heat of a Tennessee August morning, so I ended up with one-on-one lessons at a clinic price. I would have let my makeup drip down to my thighs before I complained. Besides, it quickly became clear that I needed those one-on-one lessons badly. Because what transpired in my two months of lessons and roughly four full games of golf—three on a par-three course and one on a regular course—well, it wasn't pretty.

You wouldn't think it would take so much effort. I mean, how many different things do you have to know to hit a little white ball into a little round hole?

As it turns out, you have to know a lot. It can wear a mind out. Good grief, just keeping up with the different clubs—irons, woods, wedges, putters—is a challenge, and don't even get me started on the numbers. You need a club to get you out of the sand, one to get you out of the woods, one to get you close to the hole. (I've yet to find one to get you out of a tree—and I do mean an actual tree. I shot a ball up into one, and it never came down.) Then there are different stances, different club grips, different swings, different places to have the ball in alignment with your body before you hit it. I'm convinced there are even different ways to hold your mouth.

Yet the more time I spend playing golf, the more I'm convinced that the game has something to teach us about how our hearts shut down . . . and how we can reclaim them.

Fore!

First, there is one thing in golf that is essential, one thing that determines whether or not you make a shot at all: you have to keep your eye on the ball.

It is amazing how much better you do when you don't lift your head too quickly. That's not easy for people like me who are eager to see exactly where their ball will land. But if you keep your eye on the ball, not only will you hit it straighter and get a better score; you'll also avoid ending up like the guy my husband saw out at the golf range one day. Philly was playing a solo round, and the two golfers ahead of him suddenly hollered,

"Fore!" This was followed by a loud smash and the unmistakable tinkling of broken glass.

Even if you don't engage in the sport, you probably know that *Fore!* is what golfers yell when something goes wrong. As Brent Kelley explains it:

> "Fore"—actually, *fore!*—is a word of warning yelled
> out by a golfer who has hit an errant shot. If your shot
> is in danger of hitting or landing very close to another
> player or group of players . . . (for instance, if you
> slice a ball into an adjoining fairway), you should yell
> "fore!" to warn players to watch out.[1]

In this case, the other players weren't in danger. Apparently the guy had driven the ball into the parking lot and straight into a car window. Everyone just stood there, stunned. Then the friend of the guy who had hit the ball began to laugh hysterically. "That's his car," he told Philly.

The poor golfer had hit a ball through his own window.

I'm thinking it happened because he took his eye off the ball.

This story reminds me of the passage we looked at in the last chapter. "Above all else"—what? "Guard your heart." That's the spiritual and emotional equivalent of keeping your eye on the ball. It's how we keep from damaging ourselves and others and having to scream, "Fore!" over and over in this journey of life.

Use the Right Clubs

Here's the second thing I've learned about life from golf: using the wrong club can really mess up your game.

Let me explain.

Imagine that life is a golf game. We each have one course to play. In the process of playing that course, we will encounter all kinds of situations, positive and negative. Sometimes we'll find ourselves on velvety greens, enjoying the sunshine with our companions, reveling in the clean shot we just hit (because we remembered to keep our eye on the ball). And sometimes we'll find ourselves wildly off course—in the rough, in the trees, facing shots that seem impossible, or whacking away without getting anywhere. Life is happening to us, and we've got to respond one way or the other.

Now, imagine that each of us carries a golf bag full of "clubs"—or different ways we can respond to our circumstances. Can you see it? Pick whatever color bag you choose—this is your imagination here. I'm choosing a blue-and-brown bag because those are the colors of the bag Philly bought me the first Christmas after I took up golf.

Just for the sake of argument, let's imagine that each one of us has experienced the same event in our game of life. We could have lost a parent from divorce or death when we were young. We could have experienced any number of other things. To keep the golf analogy going, you could say we all hit the ball and it landed in exactly the same place—the sand, the rough, the putting green, wherever.

Each of us, each heart, must choose the way we are going to respond to the circumstance we find ourselves in. In essence, we decide which club we are going to pick from our bag in order to move forward on the course.

Some of us choose the appropriate club for the situation. That is, we respond in a healthy, positive way. We may hurt. We may feel the bruises. We may mutter a little bit when we find ourselves in the rough or a sand bunker. But we stay honest. We gather our courage. We remember what we've been taught about keeping our eye on the ball. Then we hit the ball and move forward.

But what if we choose the wrong club? What if we pull out a response that isn't appropriate to the situation?

All clubs have their purposes, or they wouldn't be in our bags. But some are designed only for certain purposes, and they fail dismally when used in the wrong circumstances.

What if, for example, we encounter a circumstance that calls for courage and confrontation, but we pull out the pitching wedge of performance or perhaps the driver of fear? What if we panic, pull out any old club, and just start swinging? If we do that, chances are we'll find ourselves farther and farther from where we need to be, largely because of which club we used.

There are all kinds of unhealthy ways to deal with difficulty, from people pleasing to criticizing others to trying to control our circumstances or other people. Our options are endless. But every bad choice of club has something in common. It keeps us from moving forward.

Some days we may live more in our anger or our fear. Some days we may wallow in our disappointment or our addictions or our distractions. And with every poor response, we find ourselves farther and farther from the green, until our whole game is essentially shut down.

Do you see what I'm getting at here—how this golf analogy relates to the shutting down of a heart?

There are many different ways to shut down a heart, and each response manifests itself differently in our lives. That means one person's shut-down heart may look and feel completely different from another person's. One person may appear meek and depressed. Another may be aggressive and controlling. Still another may be busy and distracted. In the coming chapters, we'll be looking at some of these different hearts. But keep in mind that they're not as different as they seem. They may be lost in different sections of the course, but they're all still lost.

Keep in mind as well that any of us can switch up which reaction we use on any given day, though most of us will have a favorite club or clubs we use habitually. The clubs we use most often will determine the specific ways that our hearts shut down, where we find ourselves as a result, and what clubs are needed to reverse the process and get us back on track.

This process of choosing clubs is something we will all have to deal with on a daily basis, as long as we're in the game. We'll constantly have to reach into our bags and choose, and each choice will either keep us moving forward or eventually shut us down. Each choice, in a sense, is a matter of life and death.

Finally—and this is absolutely crucial!—the enemy is after us the entire time we're playing. He is the ultimate demented caddy.

Caddies, you see, don't just carry clubs for golfers. They're also an invaluable source of advice regarding club selection and even provide emotional support, helping players pick their spirits up after a bad shot or hole. A good caddy can make all the difference in a person's game.

But the enemy of souls does exactly the opposite. He is perpetually after us with his lies, trying to drag us down. He's constantly whispering bad advice, trying to get us to use the wrong club, suggesting that our lives will always be full of pain, so we might as well give up. And always, always trying to get us to believe falsehoods about our heavenly Father. That is his top priority, remember—to get us to believe lies about God.

To finish the game well, we must be on guard against those lies. We must make sure we remember our training and keep listening to the One who can get us to the green. And one way to do this is to understand how different choices and responses contribute to our game—that is, the state of our heart.

That's exactly what I want us to do in the coming chapters—explore the way our choices and reactions shape us and what our hearts can look like as a result. We'll look at a number of different types of shut-down hearts, each associated with one or more poorly chosen clubs. And with each one we'll explore

- what it's like to live with this particular form of a shut-down heart—how it manifests itself in our lives, what thoughts and behaviors are associated with it, and how we can recognize it;
- what kind of life experiences and responses (clubs) contribute to this heart state;
- how it relates to other kinds of shut-down hearts;
- what lie about God from the enemy, if we believe it, might cause us to shut down in this way (using a particular club); and
- what it might take to reclaim our hearts in each situation and live with carefree, surrendered hearts once again.

As we examine the different types of "clubs" and where they can take us, be keenly aware of how they interconnect and which ones your own heart gravitates toward. (Remember, most of us pull out more than one club to get ourselves out of uncomfortable situations.) My prayer is that we will begin to identify the lies the enemy is whispering—because once we recognize them, he loses so much power.

Our goal in all of this?

First, it's to learn to keep our eye on the ball, which is how we guard our hearts. We refuse to let it out of our sight. As this becomes a habit for our lives, we will get to enjoy the pleasure of a beautiful day on the course of life.

Second, our goal is to recognize the counterproductive

choices—the wrong clubs—that keep us away from the green. Understanding these choices helps us grasp the many different ways a shut-down heart can show itself in life—and also helps us make more positive choices so we can finish strong.

Finally, our goal is to begin to recognize the difference between the lies of our demented caddy and the truth of our heavenly Father. As we do this, the game of life will drastically change for us. Opportunities we think are gone forever may become available to us again.

Philly never dreamed he would play Pebble Beach. And he absolutely never dreamed he would have a wife who would walk the course with him or learn to play his favorite game. (I'm aware not every golfing husband wants a golfing wife, and that's okay.) I also never dreamed I'd have a vacation like I did that week with a man who loved me the way this man does. And neither of us would have ever experienced what we did in those moments together had we stayed in the shut-down states we were in just years before. Because we dared to change our game, we have enjoyed so much beauty, so much love, that we never thought we'd know.

I believe you have a Pebble Beach moment awaiting your heart. It might be a place where a dream is rekindled or a dream is birthed. But it will only be found if you're willing to risk grabbing your golf bag and start listening to that *dependable* Caddy.

Trust me, the first few rounds might be *ugly*! But even in major tournaments, players go through more than one round. If Tiger Woods needs four rounds to win, I'm thinking we should be willing to give ourselves the grace God has so readily made available to us . . . and keep swinging.

So I'll see you on the course. I'll be the one up in the tree, trying to find my ball. . . .

CHAPTER FOUR

THE PERFORMING HEART

Authentic Christianity should lead to maturity,
personality, and reality. It should fashion whole men
and women living lives of love and communion.
BRENNAN MANNING

I'VE LED BIBLE STUDIES for years here in Franklin, Tennessee. Being the perpetual planner and preparer that I am, I've always had all the lessons written before the study even began, so all that was left was a bit of tweaking the week prior to teaching each one.

But this time the Lord challenged me. As I began to prepare, I felt he was telling me, "Listen to your life, and I will let you know where we're going."[1]

I'm accustomed to writing fiction that way. When I start a novel, I usually have a beginning and an end in mind but no idea where we will go in the middle. I have come to enjoy the organic and often-surprising twists and turns stories take as I let the Lord unfold them for me as we go. Often in my morning time with him he reveals scenes of the story like a movie playing out in my head. It's a thrilling experience.

But I was none too thrilled about this approach for teaching lessons. In fact, I was a wreck for two weeks before the study began—such a wreck that my husband finally cornered me in the closet the Sunday before it began (yep, I was back in there) and told me, in essence, "You need to snap out of it!"

But not being prepared frightened me. What would people think of me? What if I screwed up? What if it wasn't . . . perfect?

Then I realized—that was the point!

Once again, God was letting me know there were habitual heart responses he was still working on in me . . . and *performing* was one of them. Instead of putting on a show, I was going to have to depend on the Lord for my content and direction.

Shaping the Performing Heart

A habit of performance can enter at an early age and can be a by-product of many different events in our stories. Think back to chapter 2, where we talked about some of the different ways our innocent hearts can become jaded.

Let's talk about the "family code," for example. Now this is not necessarily a negative thing. Family codes can create a powerful sense of belonging and identity. They can be helpful in teaching values and providing guidance. But family codes, whether specifically expressed or simply assumed, can also be highly restrictive because they tend to dictate

- this is how you will act;
- this is how we want people to view you;
- this is the box in which you need to dwell; and
- this is the persona you will project.

The trouble, of course, is that each *this* may be a far cry from the reality of a child's authentic heart, the way he or she has been uniquely designed and created. Yet the expectations are clear, and the pressures they create can be intense.

I was listening to Dr. Kevin Leman recently in an interview on *Focus on the Family*. He said that whenever he left the house as a child or a teen, his father would always say the same thing: "Remember, you're a Leman." For many of us, remembering we are a Jones or a Kaminski or a Sanchez has been a driving force in our lives since we were children, and it didn't necessarily take into account how God had wired us or what he had placed in our hearts. Instead we were put into a box and expected to perform. *Do it like this. Think like this. Be like this. Talk like this.* We weren't given the opportunity to think for ourselves, let alone have dreams of our own.

In my new life as a bonus mom, one of my challenges relates to the fact that three of our children were almost teenagers when I arrived on the scene. And I had never been a mom before, much less a mom to teenagers. I'd just been a "dog mom," and dogs more or less depend on you to tell them what to do. So when I came into my kids' lives, all I really knew about parenting was "sit," "go potty," and "let's go bye-bye."

I learned really quickly that you can't parent kids the way you take care of puppies. I also realized that teenagers are in this wonderful season of life where they are discovering themselves. They are testing the waters. They are dressing weird and thinking weird, and they think *you're* weird. And my responsibility is to shepherd their hearts while at the same time giving them freedom to discover all the beautiful ways in which God has gifted them. My responsibility is to help them take their unique places in the world, not to direct their every move.

In some families, unfortunately, kids never get that option. Instead they're trained, like puppies, to perform on demand. And in learning how to perform according to this family code set for them by others, the God-designed way they're created can shut down.

Families aren't the only sources of pressure to perform, of course. Many of us feel it acutely in school, especially where the rules are rigid and the approach to teaching and discipline is "one size fits all."

A friend recently told me that her son had changed dramatically since starting kindergarten. He'd always been a rambunctious, precocious little boy, but lately he had become a tyrant at home. What they discovered was that at his particular school there was a lot of pressure to be good—meaning "sit still and listen"—and very little opportunity to be physical and active. My friend's son tried very hard to be a good boy at school, but by the time he got home, all that pent-up boy energy was ready to explode. And it did—right on his parents.

I'm not saying kids should not be expected to sit quietly in school. I believe school can be an excellent tool to teach our children discipline and self-control and how the real world will work. (It should also provide playtime and opportunity for creative expression, which an alive heart allows in its life as well.) The trouble comes when rules are applied without allowing for individual needs and learning styles. In addition, the reward system for achievement—praise and awards for sports prowess, honor roll for good grades, certificates for perfect attendance, and the like—can promote in some children an almost-insatiable desire to look perfect, act perfect, or seem as if they have it all together.

Churches, sadly, can be powerful incubators for performing hearts as well. Many of us grew up in religious cultures that were far more focused on externals than internals. How we dressed, how often we attended, what programs we involved ourselves with, and what specific rules we obeyed or didn't obey received far more attention than the state of our hearts.

My dad pastored in a very legalistic denomination that has since worked hard to break free from many of its old mind-sets. But when I was growing up, things could get pretty legalistic. I remember a time when a choir from a Christian college came to sing for us. All the girls wore what we at the time called culottes, also known as split skirts.

I asked my mom, "Why are they all wearing those things?"

"Because they aren't allowed to wear pants."

Back then it was just as absurd to me as it is now—because they basically *were* pants masquerading as skirts. It wasn't a question of modesty. It was just a technical way to get around an arbitrary rule that focused rigidly on externals instead of what really mattered—the radiant witness of that wonderful choir.

And legalistic dress codes are just one example of fostering performance-driven Christianity. Almost any aspect of church life in any denomination can tempt people to perform. One church may reward intellectual performance. Another may reward those who give the most of their money or their time. One may affirm those with social status or those who seem to have their lives together, while yet another may focus on those with the most dramatic testimonies about their past lives.

In so many of our churches, I fear, we have missed that message from 1 Samuel 16:7 that the Lord doesn't see things the way we see them. Remember? "People judge by outward appearance, but the LORD looks at the heart" (NLT). I can't help but wonder how many people live performance-based lives because of how the church has treated their hearts.

Perhaps the saddest performing scenario is the one that easily develops in an abusive, neglectful, or addictive home. Abused children may come to believe that if they act a certain way, maybe Daddy's hand won't pummel them. If they're cuter or quieter or more accomplished, maybe Mother's words won't slice through their souls. If they help more around the house, maybe they'll get more attention or love or appreciation. So they shut down the way God created them and become the person who will get the results they need. People who grow up in abusive homes can become the most adept of performers, hiding their fear and anxiety and pain behind a cheerful face, a compliant personality, an array of accomplishments, or a tough facade.

Freedom to Be Authentic

Family codes, school and church pressure, dysfunctional families—any of these and more can shape a performing heart that hides its true self.

Don't misunderstand what I'm saying here. I'm not saying that it's wrong to have standards and rules and expectations for children and adults. I'm not even saying it's always unhealthy to perform. After all, good manners are a kind of performance, especially when you're first learning them. Conforming to standards of dress and conduct in an office or a classroom might be considered performing, but it is not necessarily harmful. Reining in your temper when you're angry or waiting for a better time to have a conversation could include elements of performance in that you're not acting exactly the way you feel at any given moment.

The problem with the performing heart, in other words, lies not with the performance, but with the heart.

Performance becomes a problem when it *takes the place* of authentic emotions and actions. It's a problem when it is driven by fear of rejection or mistreatment and especially when it becomes such a habit that no one, not even the performer, recognizes it for what it is.

When you're living out of a healthy heart, you may choose

to perform to make some interactions more comfortable. You may choose to adjust your actions to your environment. You may even choose to join a community theater and act a part. But when the time comes to be real, to be vulnerable, to be yourself, you can do that too, without fear.

That's a goal Philly and I have set for our parenting. We want our children to know how to act appropriately at the table or at school. We want them to consider others. But we also want them to feel absolutely free to be themselves and to recognize that who they are is safe with us. If they want to dance in the kitchen, we'll let them dance. If they want to put on a backyard play, we'll be the audience and cheer. We've decided that there will be a world out there that will tell them all the ways they'll need to perform for the rest of their lives, and Philly and I know that trap all too well. So we try to make room for our children to be themselves anytime we can.

A Man after My Own Heart

I first got to know Philly Jones over a plate of fried fish and cheese grits. Well, that was what was on *my* plate; he had pork chops. At that first encounter, he spoke with vulnerability and genuine kindness. And that really piqued my interest because I knew from experience what performers look like, and I'd had my fill of them.

Had Philly been putting on an act that evening, it would have been our last fish-and-grits outing. In fact, my ordering fried fish and cheese grits was an expression of my authentic heart. There was no salad with dressing on the side. There was no desire to order something that would make me look like I rarely ate or always shopped at Whole Foods. The truth is, I love fried food and could eat my weight in grits. There was no performance in that dinner for me. And Philly Jones will tell you that when he heard me place that order for fried fish and cheese grits, he knew he liked me.

I liked him too, and it wasn't just an ordinary kind of liking. Sitting across from him that evening, I felt the Holy Spirit whisper sweetly, "This man has the kind of heart I want for you in a man."

Believe me, I was listening. Because with all the work God had done in my heart, I knew I could never settle for anything less than the authenticity this man was offering me.

About six weeks and quite a few actual dates later, the two of us sat on his back porch one evening in rocking chairs. The September air was still sticky, but the ceiling fans above us provided a nice breeze, and the Tennessee wildlife and nearby cows provided background music. As we sat rocking, Philly said he wanted to tell me his story—the whole story, not just the little pieces he had shared on our previous dates. He felt I needed to know all of it so I could understand what might be ahead for us.

I have to admit to feeling guarded as Philly began to reveal the wounds of his fractured life. I didn't want this story. I wanted something nicer, more romantic, less honest. Yet that same still, small voice was speaking to me again. And what it said now was "This is why I showed you his heart first."

Philly, you see, was a broken man. In a lot of ways he's still a broken man, and he doesn't pretend to be otherwise. He had lived with a shut-down heart for much of his life, and it had cost him a lot, including his first marriage. But Philly had also fought with everything he had to reclaim his heart. He was willing to give me his story straight, without performance or pretense. And his willingness to be authentic laid a strong foundation for our love story.

Because I think Philly's story is so powerful, I asked him to share it with you in his own words. It's long, but I hope you'll stick with it because it paints such a beautiful portrait of what can happen when a person dares to reclaim his performing heart.

My story begins with my childhood because I think it's important to understand how my interaction with my parents set me up to develop a performing heart. But before I start, I want to acknowledge that I have two wonderful parents whom I love and cherish. I'm so thankful for the healthy relationship we enjoy today . . . because it wasn't always that way.

When I was growing up, my dad was a high school football coach in a small town in Georgia. He was a great coach and sort of a hero in the community. He was a deacon in our church and served as a father figure for many of his players who didn't have fathers. However, like many men of his generation, he was consumed with his job, which meant that in many ways he was emotionally absent from his family. That left my mom to take care of business at home.

Mom took pride in running our household and making sure my younger sister and I had what we needed, but she longed to be loved and cared for differently by my dad. I sensed her need, so in my teenage years I stepped into the role of being her "emotional spouse." I looked out for her, carried her burdens at times, and tried to make sure her feelings were taken care of.

Of course, this was unnatural and unhealthy for a kid my age, but I couldn't see that at the time. I was proud of my close relationship with my mom, but neither of us had any idea how this dysfunction was setting me up for trouble down the road. Only in recent years have I been able to understand the impact this family situation had on me.

First, as a teen, I wasn't equipped to take care of a grown woman the way a man is supposed to care for his wife. By design, I wasn't enough for her, and I felt that. I can look back now and see how my interaction with my mom birthed in me the burning questions I have wrestled with as a man: "Am I enough?" "Do I measure up?" "Am I really man enough to get the job done?"

Second, this obligation I felt to care for my mom forced me to grow up too quickly. It's a tremendous responsibility to be the man of the house, especially when you're really just a kid. There wasn't much time for childish things or the typical reckless teen behavior. As a result, I felt robbed of a part of my childhood.

Do you see the setup here? The burden I felt as a teenage boy to step into my father's man-size shoes left me questioning, overly responsible, and more than a little confused. I spent high school, college, my twenties, and my early thirties trying to prove myself by becoming a top performer at whatever I did. I strove for measurable accomplishments so I would have tangible proof that I did measure up.

This pattern had actually started in high school. During my ninth grade year, I'd told my parents I had three goals for high school: to be valedictorian, to get a football scholarship, and to have perfect attendance. I accomplished all three.

After high school, I accepted a football scholarship at Furman University and carried this same

performance mind-set with me to college. I graduated summa cum laude, served as captain of the
football team and president of the largest Christian
organization on campus, and became a finalist for the
Rhodes Scholarship.

To be clear, I didn't feel pressure from my parents
to achieve these things. My discipline and drive came
from this unhealthy desire to measure up to some
ridiculous standard I had set for myself.

Of course, I didn't realize that at the time. I was
just doing what I thought I was created to do. Can you
see the self-deception in that? I was living the truth of
Jeremiah 17:9:

> The heart is deceitful above all things
> and beyond cure.
> Who can understand it? (NIV)

This is one of the traps of the performing heart. We
convince ourselves that we can do it all—by ourselves.
"I don't need your help, thank you very much. I've got
it under control."

I'm not saying there's anything wrong with setting
goals and aiming high. There was certainly nothing
wrong with any of my specific involvements. For
me, though, my high-achievement lifestyle was the
beginning of a dangerous life pattern.

What's next for a college graduate who supposedly
has it all together, who is "mature beyond his years"?
That's right—marriage. In my distorted view, it was
time to move on to the next phase of my life. So I got

married during my senior year and secured a good job as an accountant with Arthur Andersen in Atlanta.

And the performance continued. During my first seven years of marriage, I advanced through the Andersen ranks at record pace (which required long work hours), earned the professional credentials of CFA and CPA (which required hundreds of hours of study in my spare time), had five children, and lived in five different homes (because we convinced ourselves we were making wise investments by buying and flipping homes in the then–rapidly rising Atlanta housing market).

Needless to say, my marriage suffered. I was still basically a kid, but now I had enormous responsibilities. We had financial stress, marital conflict, and unhealthy parental involvement in our marriage.

All this was overwhelming for someone in his twenties, and one of my coping mechanisms was to find unhealthy ways to escape. How many times do we hear stories of people who develop addictions out of a need to escape their pain or circumstances? Well, I can certainly relate. My life was way out of control, and my heart was dying day by day.

My wife and I eventually sought counseling and worked hard on our marriage for a number of years. We even moved to Nashville to get a fresh start in a new place, but we quickly performed our way back into some of the same old habits. Finally, after thirteen years of marriage, we divorced.

At that point, I was a broken, wrecked man who had contributed significantly to the wreckage of my wife's heart and made life difficult for my children.

I didn't even know who I was anymore. I certainly didn't feel like a man. I had proved what I feared all along: that I was not enough and that I didn't measure up.

That is where my journey to reclaim my heart began—at rock bottom. But before I could move on, I had to identify what had been lost:

- Part of my childhood had been stolen from me— my innocence, my freedom to grow up and make mistakes.

- I had missed out on so many relationships, especially in high school and college. The performing heart is so focused on maintaining the image of perfection that there's not much room for honesty or vulnerability. Performers like me tend to build impenetrable walls around our hearts to keep others out because we fear they may discover that we don't measure up. Performance becomes our hiding place.

- I had lost touch with my emotions. It got to the point where I didn't allow myself to cry or get angry or feel much of anything. I was always even-keeled. In performance there's not much room for honest emotions because emotions can be messy and uncontrollable.

- I had even lost my health. During the month following my divorce, I got sick for a week. My back went out on a business trip. Then one night I fell asleep at the wheel, ran off the road, and totaled my car. And through it all, I had a hard time keeping weight on. My body just wasn't working the way it should.

So what did I do to reclaim my heart?

First of all, I found a wonderful counselor and friend, Ken Edwards. As Denise has mentioned, he was her counselor too. We found him independently of each other, well before we even met. Ken was very instrumental in walking with me and guiding me through this journey of reclaiming my heart.

One of the first things I did after Ken and I started meeting was repent of shutting down my heart. I asked God for forgiveness for taking the perfectly healthy heart he had given me and wrecking it. I had ignored my heart and abused it. I'd set it aside and hadn't cared for it. I'd basically taken God off the throne of my heart and inserted myself because my *pride* had told me that I knew what was best for me and my *fear* told me that if anyone ever knew the real truth about me, I would be exposed. I had believed the lies of the enemy and lived in that bondage year after year, shutting God out.

So I had to recognize all this as sin, repent of it, and ask for God's forgiveness. I had to face the reality that what I feared was true: I really *am* not enough—without Christ. But that's why he died for me, so I don't have to keep pretending that I measure up.

Then I asked God to restore my heart—to give me back my emotions and allow me to feel again. I realized that the only way I could heal was to allow myself to feel all the hurt, pain, and anger I had ignored for so many years. I had to get that stuff out of me. Since then I've come such a long way in learning to feel. I also had to learn to listen to my heart again, to trust my gut. If we stay shut down too long, we lose the ability to even hear our hearts. I have learned to value my heart and respond to it when it's telling me something.

As my restoration continued, I also prayed for friends, real friends, with whom I could be honest. I remember sharing my story with someone else for the first time. I was literally shaking as I told him about my life and revealed some of the skeletons in my closet. It was a huge step for me to be that vulnerable. And I was amazed at how my friendships began to change when I stopped performing and instead presented myself as a real person with real struggles. I met Denise a few years later and told her my story—the first time I had shared it with a woman. It was a big step for me and very liberating.

For me, this has been a journey about the birth of a "new Philly"—a rebirth, if you will. One of the things I love about our God is that he is a God of second chances. He doesn't give up on us. He keeps pursuing us and wants to rescue us. According to Psalm 18:19, it's because he loves me so much that he actually "delights in me" (NLT). That's almost impossible for me to get my head around, but I'm learning to trust it—because God has shown his love for me in so many wonderful ways.

For example, it's been unbelievable for me to see the transformation in my mom and dad over the past few years. At their age, to have the courage and humility to own their dysfunction and fight for their hearts has been a blessing to see. It would have been easy for them to believe the lie that "this is just who I am." (In case you're interested, my dad is still coaching. He's the head coach at Shorter University in Rome, Georgia. Go Hawks!)

And though I love being a father to my daughters, I truly believe that one of the reasons God gave me a son is so that I could reclaim a piece of my childhood through him. I'm not talking about a sick, unhealthy way of living through your child. But it's so fun and redeeming for me to take him out on the football field or baseball field or to catch crawdads with him in the creek. It's such a gift for me to enjoy his free, adventurous boy spirit.

And to have a second chance at marriage with such a wonderful woman—that's an amazing gift. I certainly still have my wounds and scars and personal battles to fight, but God has redeemed so much of what I thought was forever lost.

To wrap up, my story began with a series of circumstances that set me up for performance, followed by years of extreme behavior and unhealthy patterns. You may have been set up too, in a different way. Your style of performance may be more subtle but just as damaging to your heart and relationships. If you haven't already, I hope you'll start the journey today to reclaim your performing heart. There's so much life yet to be lived.

The Power of an Authentic Heart

My friend, when you are willing to fight for your heart, you are only setting up those you love and those you might one day love for the most beautiful parts of you. What you have to offer them out of your authentic heart—even when it's broken—is something far more powerful than any performance you could give.

The truth is, performance stifles relationships, and the more effective the performance, the more isolated and cut off both the performer and the audience will be. It just makes sense when you think of it. If you are showing others only your performing self, you'll never have the confidence that they love your real self.

Besides, people rarely open their hearts to those who seem too perfect. They respond to people who are real and vulnerable and honest. I learned this early in my ministry. People trust me with their hearts, with their stories, because I am willing to open up to them the vulnerable and often-unpleasant parts of my own story.

Here's another big problem with depending on performance to get us through life: we'll eventually be found out. I tell people all the time that you can't hide crazy forever; sooner or later it will reveal itself. We can try to stuff down all our problems and dysfunctions in a heroic attempt to perform our way through life. It may work pretty well—for a while. But just as a geyser is sure to erupt, our "stuff" will almost certainly be exposed. God is so eager to capture our hearts that he'll do whatever he can to expose our performances and bring us out from behind the curtain. For those of us who have spent our lives as actors on the stage of life, being exposed can be painful indeed.

What's My Motivation?

Performing hearts show so many different faces to the world:

- ◆ the supermom down the street who drinks in secret
- ◆ the beloved pastor who inspires his flock but dares not admit his own doubts
- ◆ the scared kid acting tough on the playground
- ◆ the life of the party who has lost three jobs in two years

♦ the friend who can't resist telling you over and over what she or her children have accomplished

A performer's whole life is essentially a show, an act, a desperate attempt to cover up or avoid their self-doubt, their need and insecurity, the questions they have, or the pain they feel.

The motive behind a performing heart can be fear or pride. Often there are elements of both. We don't want people to know we have problems or weaknesses or issues, so we act as if we have it all together. Maybe in the past we offered up a little of ourselves here or there and were abused, mishandled, betrayed, or had our own hearts used against us, so we make sure that won't happen again. We worry about how others might view us, so we carefully control what they see. And because we've convinced ourselves we'd be rejected if people knew the real truth about us, we put a block on the truth and become what others want us to be.

Under all these motivations is a deep aversion to being vulnerable and dependent. Jan Meyers writes eloquently about this in *Listening to Love*:

Why are we so resistant to the vulnerability that Jesus surfaces in us? Maybe because experience has taught us that to be childlike means that we will be dependent and vulnerable to harm. . . . [We tell ourselves] that if we are not vulnerable, we will not be hurt and that if we are vulnerable, we will not be loved. Steel yourself to Dad's sarcasm by becoming sullen; figure out a way to get through by constantly gauging and maneuvering; put on a brave face; scoot out quickly to avoid the woman you know will have a prescription for your situation. We know we'd like to let down our defenses; the deepest recess of our hearts wants care, reassurance, companionship, love. But we've learned there are very few safe places to do so. To be childlike asks us to hold our vulnerable hearts before God as we give up on predicting or controlling how others will handle us.[2]

Such childlike vulnerability feels daunting. Terrifying. Threatening. So we choose the "brave face" and the "gauging and maneuvering." We shut down our authentic, vulnerable hearts and put on a show instead.

And shutting down our hearts, remember, is a sin based on a lie.

The Lie of the Performing Heart: "The Way God Made Me Isn't Enough"

The particular lie that those with performing hearts have swallowed is: *The way God made me isn't enough . . . so I have to fake it.* Performers perform out of a deep distrust in the way God has designed them and written their stories. A painful sense of inadequacy and vulnerability mingles with the pride and fear, driven by the nagging accusations our enemy loves to whisper in our ears.

John Eldredge and Brent Curtis describe this tactic memorably in *The Sacred Romance*:

The core of Satan's plan for each of us is not found in tempting us with obvious sins like shoplifting or illicit sex. These things he uses more as maintenance strategies. His grand tactic in separating us from our heart is to sneak in as the Storyteller through our fears and the wounds we have received from life's Arrows. . . . Counting on our vanity and blindness, he seduces us to try to control life by living in the

smaller stories we all construct to one degree or
another. He accuses God to us and us to God. He
accuses us through the words of parents and friends
and God himself. He calls good evil and evil good
and always helps us question whether God has
anything good in mind in his plans for us. He steals
our innocence as children and replaces it with a blind
naïveté or cynicism as adults.[3]

What is the enemy's goal in all this? He wants us to fire the
Author of our story and attempt the rewrites ourselves. But
when we do that—when we put together our own scripts, act
as our own director, and perform the lead as well—we miss all
the beautiful ways God desires to love us.

Isaiah describes this so vividly:

You have everything backward!
    You treat the potter as a lump of clay.
Does a book say to its author,
    "He didn't write a word of me"?
Does a meal say to the woman who cooked it,
    "She had nothing to do with this"?
ISAIAH 29:15-16, *The Message*

But that's exactly what we do when we live with a performing heart. We subscribe to the lie that what God has done in our
lives, what he wants to do, isn't good enough. We challenge the
way the Author has written our story. And in our deluded, nar-
cissistic way, we decide we can perform our way to a better one.

The issues of the performing heart are not new. Men and
women have been distrusting the way God made them and
pretending they are something different from the beginning of

time. Let's take a good look at the story of the very first humans because it really is the beginning of all our stories. We will refer to the events of Genesis 3 many times in this book because, after all, this was the moment when Satan began spreading lies about God and human hearts first began shutting down.

The serpent was the shrewdest of all the wild animals the Lord God had made. One day he asked the woman, "Did God really say you must not eat the fruit from any of the trees in the garden?"

"Of course we may eat fruit from the trees in the garden," the woman replied. "It's only the fruit from the tree in the middle of the garden that we are not allowed to eat. God said, 'You must not eat it or even touch it; if you do, you will die.'"

"You won't die!" the serpent replied to the woman. "God knows that your eyes will be opened as soon as you eat it, and you will be like God, knowing both good and evil."

The woman was convinced. She saw that the tree was beautiful and its fruit looked delicious, and she wanted the wisdom it would give her. So she took some of the fruit and ate it. Then she gave some to her husband, who was with her, and he ate it, too. At that moment their eyes were opened, and they suddenly felt shame at their nakedness. So they sewed fig leaves together to cover themselves.

When the cool evening breezes were blowing, the man and his wife heard the Lord God walking about in the garden. So they hid from the Lord God among the trees. Then the Lord God called to the man, "Where are you?"

He replied, "I heard you walking in the garden, so I hid. I was afraid because I was naked."

"Who told you that you were naked?" the LORD God asked. "Have you eaten from the tree whose fruit I commanded you not to eat?"

The man replied, "It was the woman you gave me who gave me the fruit, and I ate it."

Then the LORD God asked the woman, "What have you done?"

"The serpent deceived me," she replied. "That's why I ate it."

GENESIS 3:1-13, NLT

Can you see the performing heart at work here? Adam and Eve were unable to accept the story God had written for them. They were basically saying, "It isn't enough. We want to write this tree into it." What did they get as a result? A separation from God (sin) that led them straight into performance. They immediately found fig leaves to cover up their authentic selves.

That's exactly what we do as we settle into life with a performing heart. Even if it starts innocently, as a protective mechanism triggered by pain in childhood, once it becomes something we claim as our identity—separate from our God design—it then becomes sin. It is the lie that causes us to create a false self.

Reclaiming the Performing Heart

Are you thinking you might be tired of the stage life? Tired of the rehearsals, the endless rewrites, the loneliness of the road? Tired of the nagging fear that if people really knew you, the real you, you'd be ignored or rejected? Tired of the exhausting suspicion that you just can't trust God to get things right?

Even after a lifetime of Oscar-worthy performances, you can

finally retire from the stage. You can reclaim your performing heart.

Here's where to start: with the truth. The truth about who we really are, what our lives are really like. The truth about our inadequacy, our brokenness, our "stuff."

We can't begin to reclaim our performing hearts—or any other form of a shut-down heart—until we recognize the reality that parts of our story just aren't pretty and that, hard as we try, we will never be enough. None of our acting can take away the truth that we have issues. None of our performances can make us enough.

But Jesus is enough, and that makes all the difference.

The apostle Paul urges us:

As you therefore have received Christ Jesus the Lord, so walk in Him, rooted and built up in Him and established in the faith, as you have been taught, abounding in it with thanksgiving.

Beware lest anyone cheat you through philosophy and empty deceit, according to the tradition of men, according to the basic principles of the world, and not according to Christ. For in Him dwells all the fullness of the Godhead bodily; and you are complete in Him, who is the head of all principality and power.

COLOSSIANS 2:6-10

Did you get that? In Christ we are complete, which means that without him we'll always be incomplete. How can we ever be enough if we hang on to our performing hearts and refuse to allow him to write our story? We can't.

And as for our brokenness, our issues, our stuff—well, Jesus *specializes* in people with stuff. In fact, have you ever checked out his lineage? We're talking prostitutes, adulterers, murderers, schemers—all part of the big story of God's redemptive work in our world. But we cannot be part of that story until we're willing to own the reality of our lives—stuff and all.

This ownership step is actually the necessary starting place for reclaiming any form of shut-down heart, and we'll return to it again and again. I call this step *recognition*. Recognition means being brave enough to recognize where we are, confronting the truth of our reality.

But simply recognizing the reality of where our choices have brought us is just a first step. In order to reclaim a heart, *repentance* must follow. Remember, I said in chapter 2 that handing our hearts over is a sin, and there is no remedy to sin without repentance. When we repent, we don't just acknowledge sin. We actually decide to do life differently, with God's help. We make the conscious choice that the old patterns of behavior we have walked in are going to be a thing of the past. We are not going to be the personification of "crazy"—a person doing the same thing the same way, expecting a different result. Instead, we are choosing to do the hard work—the heart work—of moving in a different direction.

And then, in order for the change to "stick," repentance must be strengthened by *reflection* on the Word of God. Spending regular time in the Word—reading, studying, meditating, and journaling thoughts—retrains our way of thinking. It is what produces in us the change. When we replace the lies we have believed with the truth of God's Word and make a point to reflect on that truth daily, then it will begin to reflect itself in us and through us. Our lives become a reflection of his life. Our thoughts become a reflection of his thoughts for us. Our hearts become a reflection of his heart.

These "three Rs"—recognition, repentance, and reflection—

are central to the process of reclaiming a performing heart or any shut-down heart. But there's another step that's just as important: telling our story.

The Story of Our Lives

Telling your story doesn't mean you have to make the talk show circuit or write a tell-all book. And telling your story doesn't mean you have to tell everyone else's along with it. It certainly doesn't mean you have to trash others in the process. You can be honest and still honor others. The key is to focus on your part of the story, to claim the pieces that belong to you and to claim the freedom to share your story when you know someone needs what only that story can offer them.

I often sit with my sweet husband as he encounters a heart that could be ministered to by his story. I listen as he freely unveils his faults, his sins, his stuff. And I watch as the person's heart is touched and changed by his willingness to give up worrying about what people might think of him and to be completely okay with the way God is writing his story. Daring to do that can truly liberate you—and it can set other people free as well.

Do you know why the enemy fights so intensely to convince us that God didn't make us enough? It's because he knows the power of our stories. In fact, they have the power to destroy him.

Sounds crazy, doesn't it—that our stories can have that much impact? Well, doesn't it make sense that if the enemy is going to fight so hard to keep us from living our authentic lives and to convince us that our Father, the Creator of our very hearts, didn't make us enough, there must be something he has to gain from doing so? Remember, the enemy is all about self-preservation.

Look at the potential power of your story lived out authentically—revealed to John in the book of Revelation:

Then I heard a loud voice shouting across the heavens,

"It has come at last—
    salvation and power
and the Kingdom of our God,
    and the authority of his Christ.
For the accuser of our brothers and sisters
    has been thrown down to earth—
the one who accuses them
    before our God day and night.
And they have defeated him by the blood of the Lamb
    and by their testimony.
And they did not love their lives so much
    that they were afraid to die."
REVELATION 12:10-11, NLT (EMPHASIS ADDED)

Oh, my friend, what a powerful revelation to our hearts. The enemy, the accuser of you and me, is defeated by our testimonies, by our stories. Every time we share our honest testimony—not the story of what we wish we were, what we wish people would see, what we want people to think about us, but the real story of the pain we've felt, the difficulties we've overcome, and the God who brought us through—we demolish the lie that the way God made us isn't enough. We get to the place where we don't care how other people perceive us or how they treat us. We stop holding on to our lives so carefully and dare to live in his abundance, giving God the glory and, in the process, participating in the enemy's ultimate destruction.

Living in God's Story

Like many others with shut-down hearts, I was once a consummate performer. I would walk around in my designer clothes with my tidy little haircut and my cute Southern ways, and you would never know how messed up I was inside. Then God shattered the pride that had kept me performing. When I was sitting with the rubble of my marriage at my feet, there was nowhere to hide. My broken story was there for anyone to see.

Crises have a way of doing that. When you're checking into a rehab center, there is nowhere to hide. When you're in a Celebrate Recovery class, there is nowhere to hide. When you're sitting at your window watching someone repossess your car, there is nowhere to hide. But that can be a good thing—if we have the humility to face the truth about our lives. Because when you've lived your life performing perfectly, realizing how unworthy you really are and how worthy God is can create a heart of worship in you that changes everything for the better.

Many of us have lived our lives with a perspective like the Pharisee named Simon, who invited Jesus over to his house. "Isn't Jesus lucky he gets to hang out with me?" But the real perspective we should have when it comes to Jesus should be like the prostitute who walked into Simon's house that same day and emptied her alabaster perfume box, the only thing of value she had, onto Jesus' feet. Her heart said, "Knowing you, loving you, is worth everything I have."

God has an amazing story he desires to write for you. A story better than *Gladiator* or *Gone with the Wind*, filled with wonder and beauty and adventure. And he wants you to live it, not perform it. If we limit ourselves to a paltry existence of writing and performing only the story we want other people to see, we will leave no room for the real, authentic story the Author of our days is writing for us. Until you and I are willing to stop acting as if we've got it all together and to empty ourselves of all that we are, we will miss what the Father has in mind for us.

The true story of our lives—straight from the heart.

CHAPTER FIVE

THE DISAPPOINTED HEART

*Disappointment to a noble soul is what cold water is to burning
metal; it strengthens, tempers, intensifies, but never destroys it.*

ELIZA TABOR

TEARS FELL DOWN HER FACE right in the middle of the busy
Nashville deli. I let my Reuben sandwich grow cold as the
woman across from me shared her sadness about being a few
months shy of her fortieth birthday and still single. Her last
close friend was about to walk down the aisle, leaving her feeling
incredibly alone. And hopelessly, excruciatingly disappointed.

The very next evening I talked with another good friend, a
young husband and father Philly and I have known for years.
He had hoped to have "made it" professionally by now—the
big office, the big title, the big paycheck. But the last few years
had brought him unfulfilled dreams, unmet expectations, and
challenges bigger than he had thought he would face. At that
moment he felt like his whole life was a disappointment.

The next day it was a phone call. Even on the cell, I could

feel every ounce of my friend's pain. She had lived virtually every one of her thirty years with the knowledge that her own mother had not wanted her—not when she was little and apparently not now either. Every day she continues to live with a deep and gaping wound of disappointment, her heart longing for a response she will never get.

We all know disappointment. In fact, most of us experience it on some level every day.

Most of the disappointments are little. They're one-time incidents, easy to shake off. But other disappointments loom large. People we trust let us down. Our hopes and dreams don't pan out. The picture we painted in our heads of what our lives would be just doesn't match up with what our real lives are like.

The beautiful thing about God is he affirms to us that disappointment is real. He validates what we're feeling. Time after time he tells us that he gets it.

- "Unrelenting disappointment leaves you heartsick" (Proverbs 13:12, *The Message*).
- "A cheerful heart is good medicine, but a broken spirit saps a person's strength" (Proverbs 17:22, NLT).
- "The human spirit can endure a sick body, but who can bear a crushed spirit?" (Proverbs 18:14, NLT).
- "A sad heart makes it hard to get through the day" (Proverbs 15:13, *The Message*).

Verses like that are the Father's sweet way of letting us know our feelings of disappointment are normal. We don't have to pretend they don't exist. It's impossible to get through life without being let down from time to time—and being sad about it.

But what happens when disappointment settles in on us like a farmer's rain—that slow, steady, soaking kind? Perhaps it begins with the loss of a spouse or a child or a dream, leaving us despondent. Perhaps we experience the snowball effect of one disappointment after another—a lost job results in the loss of a home, which brings on a marital or health crisis. Or perhaps the same disappointment will chip away at us year after year after year, as in the case of my friend who longs for a husband, the woman who longs for a mother's approval, or a spouse who encounters rejection in the bedroom night after night.

After a while it doesn't seem to matter if it's several things or a thousand of the same things. Disappointment becomes the *only* thing. That is how a heart shuts down and becomes a disappointed heart, now funneling all of life through the experience of disappointment. As if this is the whole of our story instead of only part of our story. As if the only thing we can expect out of life is to be let down again and again, so there's no point in planning for the future or hoping for anything.

And that's exactly where the enemy wants us to live— perpetually discouraged, perpetually defeated, convinced that this is how we'll feel for the rest of our lives. The enemy's goal is to keep us focused on this place of disappointment. Because focusing on disappointment removes our ability to see all the places in our lives where God is moving. We allow our hearts to live in the place where we have convinced ourselves he *isn't* moving.

On the morning after my divorce was final, I prayed, "Lord, whatever you do, don't let me miss you." I had taught on pain and experienced enough pain of my own to know that it can be deafening. Pain screams, and when it's screaming, it's hard to focus on anything else.

But I also knew that God was present and available in the middle of my pain, and I didn't want to miss that presence. So my next statement was a declaration to the enemy and the deceiver of my soul. I said, "You may have stolen my marriage, but you will not rob me of one more day of my life."

I can't begin to tell you all the ways I saw God love me in my details over the following days and weeks and months, once I resolved not to keep my focus only on my pain and disappointment.

I remember a time after my divorce when I really, really needed a haircut but just didn't have the money for one. Money was tight, and every cent in my bank account had been spoken for that month. I had even tried trimming my own hair. (Note to the broke: if you're at this point, at least try to find a friend who can do this for you!)

One evening during that time I went over to my brother and sister-in-law's house to babysit my niece Georgia. While I was there, my sister-in-law kind of tossed a piece of paper at me.

I eyed it curiously. "What is this?"

"It's a coupon for a free haircut at the Rodney Gaven Salon. It was in our goody bags from that fashion show we went to, and somehow your coupon got put into my bag."

I gaped at her. That had been three months earlier—and three months ago I hadn't needed a haircut.

On my way home that night, I thanked the Lord over and over and over—then called for an appointment. I remember the day I went to that salon to get my hair cut. It might have been the most beautiful haircut I've ever had—because it felt as if the Lord had cut my hair.

That may sound a little silly to you, but I honestly believe God shows us his love this way—day by day, minute by minute, in all sorts of thoughtful and detailed ways. But the narrow focus of a disappointed heart will make us miss these love gestures every time. We stop expecting good things to happen, so we don't even recognize them when they're right in front of us.

It's no sin to be disappointed or discouraged, but it's a sin to live with a disappointed heart, blind to everything but the ways that life has let us down.

The Lie of the Disappointed Heart: "God Is Not *for* Me"

If you just read the story about my haircut and your first thought was *God would never do that for me,* then you have pretty much encountered the lie behind the disappointed heart.

The disappointed heart assumes *God isn't* for *me.* Not in the sense of "God just isn't my cup of tea," but in the sense of "God isn't on my side." This lie assumes that God doesn't care enough to come through for me. That is another perfect example of how "the accuser of our brothers and sisters" attacks the hearts and minds of God's children.

We have a child who loves to announce, "That's not fair!" What she really means, of course, is "That's not what I want."

And we, like all parents, answer her with the age-old response, "Life's not fair."

We're right, of course. The truth is, Adam and Eve messed up fairness. They hijacked it for all of us. All fairness ended with their sin. Since the Garden, there hasn't been anything fair about living in the world, and a lot of our disappointment stems from that fact. Still, many of us hold on to the hope that God is fair—that he can be trusted to do what is right. And the Bible tells us just that—God is a God of justice.

But this reality gets all twisted when the enemy's lies start working on our disappointment, convincing us that *right* and *fair* are synonymous with "what I want." Then, when life doesn't go the way we have planned or expected, we end up even *more* disappointed because "it's not fair" or "it's not right." Like children, we feel unloved and mistreated simply because we haven't gotten our own way.

Where did this childish misconception originate? All the way back in the Garden—even before Adam and Eve's disobedience ended fairness in the world. It happened right after God looked at Adam and Eve and said, "You can have anything in this garden but one thing" (see Genesis 2:16-17).

Who couldn't live with that? "You can have the whole world. Just stay away from that one tree." Were Adam and Eve crazy? I mean, I think I could cope with staying away from just *one* forbidden thing if I had so much else—the ocean and the mountains and animals to hang out with and grass between my toes and blue sky above my head, a husband made by the very hands of God, lots of great fruit to eat, and God himself to walk and talk with. I could forgo a single tree.

Of course I'm coming at this with the knowledge of what has come before me. Until that moment Adam and Eve had never known temptation. But still, the enemy was crafty. He approached Adam and Eve with a lie designed to confuse them about the difference between what is right and what is fair. He planted a doubt that in turn created a sense of entitlement, a spirit that has permeated every generation since Adam and Eve and has seemed to be unleashed as if on steroids in the generation we live in now.

It started with a question from the serpent to Eve: "Did God really say you must not eat the fruit from any of the trees in the garden?"

She answered with what God had told her: that they could eat from all the trees except one and that, according to God, they would die if they ate from the forbidden tree.

What did the serpent say? "You won't die! . . . God knows that your eyes will be opened as soon as you eat it, and you will be like God, knowing both good and evil" (Genesis 3:1-5, NLT).

And there's the lie. Did you see it? He was basically telling her, "God has set you up. He is holding out on you. If he really cared about you, if he were really *for* you, he'd let you have anything in this garden. But he doesn't. Why? Because he doesn't want you to be like him. If he really loved you, he would *want* you to have everything he has."

As you know, the lie worked. Eve and Adam both bought the serpent's slander of God. They both ended up doing exactly what God had told them not to do:

> The woman . . . saw that the tree was beautiful and its fruit looked delicious, and she wanted the wisdom it would give her. So she took some of the fruit and ate it. Then she gave some to her husband, who was with her, and he ate it, too. At that moment their eyes were opened, and they suddenly felt shame at their nakedness. So they sewed fig leaves together to cover themselves.
>
> GENESIS 3:6-7, NLT

The lie the serpent told the first humans at the beginning of time hasn't changed much. It's packaged a little differently now, but it's the same spirit, and it still breeds a dangerous sense of entitlement. The enemy is still trying to convince us that God isn't being fair to us, that he doesn't have our best interests at heart, and that we should have anything that "looks good." The more we fall for that lie, the more disappointment we'll experience, and the more our hearts are likely to shut down.

Now please hear me. I am not discounting your disappointment. I know what disappointment looks like and feels like. I have lived it for many years, under many different circumstances. And as I've indicated, it's normal to feel sad and discouraged when people let us down or when life doesn't live up to our expectations. In fact, there's probably something wrong with us if we don't feel down under those circumstances.

But what I am trying to explain is how the enemy maneuvers in our disappointment, how he is the one who sets us up and causes us to miss the beautiful gifts of our loving Father—the Father who created Eden for us, a place where he could fellowship with us in a personal and intimate way; the Father who kept loving and pursuing us even after we messed up our relationship with him; the Father who sent his Son to die for us and who continues to love us and woo us back to him through the smallest details of our lives. This is a God who goes way beyond fair, showing us mercy and grace when we deserve it the least. I don't know about you, but to me that is wonderful news because if life were really fair, a lot of us would be in trouble.

Yet it is the enemy of our souls who still gets into our heads and hearts and convinces us that if life isn't working out the way we pictured it, that means God doesn't care about us. What a sneaky lie. First he convinces us that we are entitled to something, that our life is "supposed" to go a certain way. Then, when it doesn't happen, we are left with a disappointed heart.

And boy, the entitlement thoughts we have! We feel entitled to be married. We feel entitled to have children. We feel entitled to have parents who love us, friends who treat us exactly the way we want them to, work that fulfills us. That's the way it's supposed to be, isn't it? Is God holding out on us? Shouldn't we be entitled to eat of *all* the trees in this garden? Shouldn't we be able to have anything that looks good?

Remember, the forbidden tree was "beautiful." It looked good, just as being married looks good, having children looks good, keeping our home, our retirement, and our health looks good. When we buy into the lie of entitlement, losing any of these "good" things really throws us. So when a prayer we've prayed isn't answered the way we think it should be or when life offers us something different from the happily ever after we've dreamed up for ourselves, we are left with only one conclusion: *God isn't* for *me*. And that's when our hearts collide with disappointment.

But there is an alternative to entitlement thinking. It involves widening our view a little. Could it be that God hasn't let us down, but the enemy has set us up by urging us to buy into a narrow and shallow picture of how life should look? Could it be that a loving God has something more for us than what we think we want?

My friend, I am here today to tell you that God will not always show up the way that looks best to you or to me. He's got a much wider perspective than that, and his purposes for us involve so much more than making us feel good or giving us what we think we want. It's almost a cliché in Christian circles these days, but it's still true: God is far more concerned with our character than he is with our comfort.

You might want to read that line again: God is far more concerned with our character than he is with our comfort.

Romans 5 tells us that "suffering produces perseverance; perseverance, character; and character, hope" (vv. 3-4, NIV). That passage makes it clear that God is okay with allowing suffering in our lives, that bad experiences can ultimately have good results if we will allow it. God is after our hearts—our whole hearts, without reserve. He wants us to love and trust him in the deepest parts of us, and sometimes it takes suffering to get us to that point.

But—and this is important—he promised to be with us always. Not just in the future, in heaven, but right here, right now, in the middle of our messy and disappointing lives. And that gift of God's constant presence in our lives makes such a difference. The words of David are still true for us today: "I would have lost heart, unless I had believed that I would see the goodness of the LORD in the land of the living" (Psalm 27:13).

God still has good things for us in the middle of our pain. I would lose hope too if I didn't believe that. But I know he is with us and moving even in our deepest places of sorrow, in the sad, barren places of our disappointment, doing whatever is necessary to make us his.

Even when he tells us no.

When God Says No

We're told in 2 Corinthians 12:7 that the apostle Paul lived for many years with a "thorn" in his flesh. We don't know exactly what that thorn was. It could have been physical. It could have been a person or a life circumstance. Honestly, I think one of the beautiful things about not knowing is that I can imagine my own "thorn" in Paul's story. But what we do know is that Paul asked God three times to remove this trouble that continued to plague him.

How did God respond to Paul's fervent prayers?

He said no.

What? The God of the universe said no to a prayer?

Yes, sometimes God says no. Sometimes when we're claiming our healing, God says no. Sometimes when we're longing for children, God says no. Sometimes when we desire a spouse, God says no. Sometimes when we pray for something to be saved, restored, given, God says no in ways that feel heartbreaking and deeply disappointing.

Why? Because he is after something greater than anything we could know on this earth. He is after the eternal value of our hearts. "What we suffer now is nothing," Paul wrote, "compared to the glory he will reveal to us later" (Romans 8:18, NLT).

God reveals himself in glorious ways through pain and suffering. This book would not exist without the disappointments of my own heart and my hard battle to reclaim it. And God wants to put your disappointments to good use as well. He wants you to allow him to reclaim your story, paint over your lost picture, and provide for you all the wondrous elements of his strength in your weakest places. Our disappointments can offer us the extreme privilege of seeing God in ways we've never seen him before. He tells us clearly, "For my thoughts are not your thoughts, neither are your ways my ways" (Isaiah 55:8, NIV).

But aren't you glad? I am. I wouldn't want God to think like I do. I wouldn't want a God reduced to my humanness. My frivolity. My pettiness. My warped sense of fairness.

I want a God bigger than I am. No, I *need* a God bigger than I am, especially when I've been disappointed, when life isn't working out like I wanted it to. What a comfort to know that my heavenly Father knows better than I do. And like any good parent, there will be times when he can and will say no. This means there will be some things in life we will never understand. We just have to settle our hearts around that. Sometimes he removes our "thorns," and sometimes he allows them to remain, and in both he shows us—whether we choose to see it or not—just how much he really cares.

Paul writes his response to God's no. "Three times I pleaded with the Lord to take it away from me. But he said to me, 'My grace is sufficient for you, for my power is made perfect in weakness'" (2 Corinthians 12:8-9, NIV).

Look at our Father's response to Paul's repeated plea. It was a no, but it wasn't an angry no. In fact, he was offering Paul a revelation of himself, a revelation of something bigger than Paul's temporary condition. He was offering him a picture of how big God is. "*My* grace is enough for you, Paul. But even more than that, it is perfected in your place of weakness."

In other words, "Paul, if you will allow me, I'm going to let you encounter me in a way you never have before—and I'm going to do it in the area that is so painful for you, where you feel so weak. I am offering you perfection in your most inadequate places."

What a trade-off—God's strength for all my countless inadequacies and his grace for living with the disappointment of those times when he says no.

Reclaiming the Disappointed Heart

The question, of course, is how we can go about appropriating God's sufficient grace for a disappointed heart. I believe the place to start is where reclaiming each heart begins—with recognition, repentance, and reflection.

We must recognize the lie the enemy has convinced us of—the lie that God's not *for* us, that he's not on our side, that he doesn't care. Romans 8 gives us the perfect words:

> If God is for us, who can be against us? He who did
> not spare His own Son, but delivered Him up for us all,
> how shall He not with Him also freely give us all things?
> Who shall bring a charge against God's elect? It is God
> who justifies. Who is he who condemns? It is Christ
> who died, and furthermore is also risen, who is even at
> the right hand of God, who also makes intercession for
> us. Who shall separate us from the love of Christ? Shall
> tribulation, or distress, or persecution, or famine, or
> nakedness, or peril, or sword? As it is written:
>
> "For Your sake we are killed all day long;
> We are accounted as sheep for the slaughter."

Yet in all these things we are *more than conquerors* through Him who loved us. For I am persuaded that neither death nor life, nor angels nor principalities nor powers, nor things present nor things to come, nor height nor depth, nor any other created thing, shall be able to separate us from the love of God which is in Christ Jesus our Lord.

vv. 31-39 (emphasis added)

This is the truth that the disappointed heart can stand on. It can declare to God, in order to confront the lie of the enemy and its own brokenness, "I may not understand it. But I know you are working good out for everything that concerns me. You are *for* me, and nothing can ever separate me from that reality!"

What comes next? Once we've recognized the lie and embraced the truth, we can start working on handling our inevitable disappointments in a healthier way. For instance, we can learn the power of adjusting our expectations.

What Do You Expect?

I remember the day when Philly and I went on our first golf outing together. I had it all planned. I'd bring my golf notes, get a large McDonald's Coke and put it in the drink slot of the pull cart, and enjoy a leisurely round of golf with my husband. Well, I forgot the notes, so we had to go back for those. Philly forgot his golf shoes. By that time, we were already a little frazzled.

He's a pretty discerning fellow, so he posed the question as we headed back to the golf course for the second time: "So, babe, what are your expectations for today?"

That made me stop. I hadn't realized I had any expectations until he asked. And in pondering the question, I realized that I had a choice of what to expect. If my expectation was for everything to go perfectly, chances were that I would be disappointed. So I regrouped.

"I would love to hit the ball more than I miss it. I would love to not take out a car window in the process. And most of all, I would love to have fun with you." Then I asked him, "What are your expectations?"

He paused for a minute before answering in that calm manner he has. "I am expecting this to be a long game of golf."

We both laughed. But do you know, neither of us left the course disappointed that day. True, my first three swings on the driving range missed completely and caused the girl behind me to laugh. But I still told my husband when we climbed into the car, "That was one of the best days I've had with you since we've been married."

To which he replied, "You did a lot better than I thought."

That's the power of adjusting expectations. Sometimes just stepping back and taking a more realistic view can save a lot of disappointment. I wasn't giving up on my expectations, but I was opening myself to the reality expressed in Psalm 62:5-6:

> My soul, wait only upon God and silently submit to
> Him; for my hope and expectation are from Him. He
> only is my Rock and my Salvation; He is my Defense
> and my Fortress, I shall not be moved (AMP).

You see, there is a difference—a big difference—between feeling *entitled* to something from God and having our expectation and hope come from him. One is about our picture of the way life should be. The other is about God's picture for us. And that is where the disappointed heart must come to a place of surrender—surrendering entitlement for hope in the Lord.

I can hold on to my Pollyanna expectations—my personal

sense of what is supposed to happen—and be disappointed every time. But if I choose instead to place my expectations in my heavenly Father—believing he'll show up, write the story *he* desires to write, and provide what is needed for that to happen—he'll never let me down.

Making Friends with Forgiveness

Adjusting expectations can make a big difference to a disappointed heart. But if we really want to move past the disappointments that shut us down, we also have to make forgiveness our friend.

Whom do we need to forgive? Often it's another person who has hurt us or let us down—a friend, a family member, someone we go to church with, a coworker, even a stranger who treated us poorly. Until we can manage to forgive that person, the pain of the disappointment is likely to linger.

Sometimes forgiveness doesn't involve other people. At some time in our lives, most of us will encounter the need to forgive ourselves. We need to receive the forgiveness God has given us for our past mistakes and failures and release ourselves from the poor decisions that might have gotten us where we are. This isn't always as easy as it sounds. Our pride can get in the way, or we may fear we're being soft on our own sin. But the more we can learn to give ourselves the same grace we offer to others— the sufficient grace from our Father that finds its strength in weakness—the more freedom we'll have from the debilitating effects of disappointment.

For some of us, there may even be times when we need to forgive God, strange as that might sound. Not that God needs our forgiveness. But we may have to consciously let go of resentment we've built up toward him, just as we let go of resentment toward a person we forgive. We probably also need to release God from our expectations and ask him to forgive us for being angry with him when he hasn't done life according to what we expect.

Some of us have spent years holding on to our wounds—our anger, our bitterness, our disappointment. Forgiveness is a way to let go of all that accumulated pain. Even better, learning to forgive as we go along can prevent bitterness from lingering and settling over us.

But forgiveness, honest forgiveness, is rarely a simple, one-time choice. It's more like a golf swing that gets better as we practice. Sometimes we have to try it again and again. But when we feel that release and watch the ball of our forgiveness make its way toward the green, the sweetness in that moment will make us want to do it over and over again.

Praying through Disappointment

Prayer is another important tool for reclaiming a disappointed heart. Nearly half of the Psalms are essentially David's prayers, and I love how real they are. They seem to flow from a completely alive heart that feels free to say anything to God, knowing that God can handle the deepest places of the psalmist's pain and brokenness. David's not afraid to contradict himself either, and his mood swings can be extreme. One moment he is begging God to strike down all his enemies. The next moment he is asking God to search him and find any evil that is inside him.

I can relate to that, can't you? One minute I'm livid with the injustice of my disappointment, and the next minute I'm humbled and overwhelmed by the kindness God shows me in the middle of all my own acts of injustice. And as I lay these contradictory emotions before my Father, the real gift is found. Those real and often-raw conversations with God strengthen my disappointed heart.

But you may be at a point where that kind of dialogue with God just seems beyond you. "I can't pray," you may say. "I'm hurting too much. I don't have any words for what I'm feeling."

I understand that too. I've been there. But remember that removing us from this intimate connection with our Father is the enemy's goal, and he's good at it. He did it with Adam and Eve. He talked them into disobeying God, they gave in to the temptation, and then they were so ashamed that they hid. That's exactly where Satan wanted them, huddled in the bushes. And he wants us to respond to our disappointment by hiding from God too.

Paul knew what it was like to hurt so deeply that he couldn't even form words into a prayer. But he also learned:

> The Spirit . . . helps in our weaknesses. For we do not know what we should pray for as we ought, but the Spirit Himself makes intercession for us with groanings which cannot be uttered. Now He who searches the hearts knows what the mind of the Spirit is, because He makes intercession for the saints according to the will of God. And we know that all things work together for good to those who love God, to those who are the called according to His purpose.
>
> ROMANS 8:26-28

Sometimes there really are no words for what we're feeling. Sometimes the pain of disappointment runs so deep that all we can do is wail, cry, and groan. But God can handle that, just as he can handle our words of anger, pain, discouragement, or despair. There is not one thing we can say to him that will knock him off his throne. And when we can't say anything, the Holy Spirit, our advocate, intercedes for us with each inarticulate utterance, and in his intercession he prays the perfect will of our Father. For that to happen, though, we still have to be willing to open those places of our hearts and share them with him in intimate exchange.

You may even need to stop reading right now and allow yourself to feel all the disappointment you've gone through, then bring it to God. It's okay if it's messy. It's okay if there are no words. It's okay if you groan. Because in that real and desperate place, the Spirit is interceding on your behalf. And what a beautiful gift that is.

The Power of Praise

Did you know you can wear heaviness? Don't believe me? Go look at some pictures of yourself in the most painful seasons of your life. Can you see it? The weight on the furrowed brow? The tired eyes? Disappointment can wear us out. But the Bible tells us it's possible to exchange "the garment of praise for the spirit of heaviness" (Isaiah 61:3). If we can do that, we'll take another step toward reclaiming a disappointed heart.

Praise is what reminds us of who God is, what he has done, and what he will continue to do. Disappointment keeps our eyes focused on us, but praise moves our eyes up to our Father and all the power he encompasses. That is what Adam and Eve should have done in the face of the enemy's lies. I really believe that if they'd stopped and praised God for who he is, what he had done, and what he had given them, they would have forgotten the lone tree they lacked.

One day a week I set aside my prayer time for nothing but praise. I don't ask God for anything unless there is an immediate need, and even then I try to word the request as praise. I've come to believe that praise should be a lifestyle.

Why does praise matter so much? One reason is that bitterness and resentment cannot cohabit with praise, so they either resist it or flee. I have certainly found that true in my life. The more I praise, the less room I have in my heart for disappointment. Praise also helps me widen my vision and look past my narrow desires and my limited view of what I think my life is supposed to be like. And it helps me release my entitlement. That's especially important because living with a spirit of entitlement can actually cause me to miss God—because God is not going to perform for me. But living with a heart of praise makes it far easier to encounter God and see him at work.

One of my favorite ways to keep praise in my life is through singing. I find it a helpful tool for reclaiming a disappointed heart. The Psalms are filled with references to singing. In fact, the Psalms *are* songs.

- ◆ "Sing praise to Your name, O Most High" (9:2).
- ◆ "Sing praises to the LORD" (9:11, 27:6, and 68:32).
- ◆ "I will sing to the LORD" (13:6 and 104:33).
- ◆ "Sing to Him a new song" (33:3).

Paul and Silas sat in a jail cell convicted of something they didn't do. And it was while they were singing that their chains fell off and the doors flew open. Somehow God can use our singing to break us loose from the things that hold us captive.

Don't think this only works for people who can carry a tune. My husband, who probably wouldn't be chosen to stand in for Michael Bublé, has still found worship and singing to be a powerful tool to combat his disappointment. He had an iPod Nano in his bathroom drawer for a few years, and it drove the kids crazy that he was letting it sit there without being used. So for Christmas, I dug the iPod out of his drawer, loaded it up with worship music, and put it in his stocking.

Not long after that, Philly drove the kids back to their mom's. They'd been with us for two whole weeks, and I knew their leaving was hard on him. He was really hurting from the disappointment of not being with them all the time. So I called and asked him how he was doing. He said he had just dropped the kids off and was listening to his iPod. He said he needed God in the pain of that moment, so he was just driving and singing along. Worshiping—to ease his disappointed heart.

That is the power worship holds. It turns our eyes off of our pain and onto the capability of our loving, able Father.

Reframing the Picture

Recognition, repentance, and reflection, plus adjusting expectations, learning to forgive, turning to God in prayer, and practicing praise (especially singing!)—all these are important ways to reclaim a disappointed heart. But it's not a one-time process because disappointment will always be part of our lives.

Philly and I, for instance, have experienced ongoing disappointment in our new life as a blended family. One of the ways we have learned to deal with it is something Ken taught us called "reframing." Here's how Philly explains it:

> For me, the most painful part of divorce is not being
> with our kids all the time. The way my custody/
> visitation agreement is set up, the kids are with
> us approximately 40 percent of the time. I stretch
> this as far as I can by coaching their sports teams,
> volunteering at their schools, teaching their Sunday
> school classes, attending their activities, having date
> nights, etc. But no matter how hard I try, the reality
> is that I'm not their primary guardian. This means I'm
> not there on many afternoons when my son wants to

go outside and toss the football around. I'm not there most evenings when they all sit down for dinner. I'm not there every morning to send them off to school or every night to tuck them in.

Of course, there's pain and loss in this for the kids too, and they are each learning to process their own pain and disappointment. But for me, the disappointment boils down to the fact that this is not my picture of what I wanted fatherhood to look like. Every time I return them to their mom after a weekend together or drop them off at school, that wound of disappointment is pricked. That disappointment never goes away. Fatherhood is my highest calling in life, and so often I feel handicapped by my circumstances.

The irony in this experience for me is that, while my time with my kids has been diminished, my impact has actually been increased. I want to be careful that there's no self-deception in this, but I really have come to believe it's true.

I call it reframing. The point is that once I surrendered this situation to God, he reframed it for me. He has redeemed it by focusing me on impact instead of time. This is something I can live with. It's how I remember that God is *for* me in this seemingly no-win situation. But I never would have gotten to this point if I had allowed the pain of disappointment to shut me down.

I've already shared how I (Denise) lived for years with a chronically disappointed heart. My entire first marriage consisted of one disappointment after another, a seemingly endless series of "no" answers. And that wasn't what I wanted at all.

I wanted a yes—a loud yes. I wanted sixty years on the front porch. I wanted to be chosen and valued. I wanted to see myself in the faces of my children and grandchildren. I wanted a shared history and a shared love.

That was what I had always pictured our life to be. But that's not how the picture turned out. Instead I ended up in front of a judge who declared my marriage null and void. A piece of paper declared that the past thirteen years had been nothing but a charade. But if they were, they were my charade. To my disappointed heart, those thirteen years were as real as the divorce papers I held in my hand.

Then God wrote another piece of my story, and once again he challenged my picture of how my life should be. This time it was my mental image of the man I thought God needed to bring me. One day God invited me to let go of that expectation too. That was frightening, and it took a while, but I finally surrendered to what the Lord was asking.

What happened next felt like a miracle. In place of the man I thought I needed, God gave me a broken man who was fighting with everything he had to reclaim his fractured heart. When he placed this man in my life, God didn't meet my expectations; he exceeded them. Then he outdid himself by adding five wonderful children to the picture.

Amazing, right? A miracle indeed. But even in the midst of all our joy, disappointment was still close at hand. The family wedding portrait that hangs on our wall shows all seven of us dressed in khaki and white, holding hands. It's beautiful, and I love it. But five minutes before it was taken, Philly had to console the grieving heart of a child who was still longing for Mom and Dad to reconcile.

I love the concept of reframing because it's still what must happen almost daily in our life together. Again and again, we all must surrender what we thought our life would look like, surrender what we want it to look like, and face and surrender our disappointment. Then we must let God reframe the picture for us.

There are definitely still disappointments for me. In some ways this new journey is far more challenging than my first marriage. My current experience of motherhood certainly looks nothing like the picture I had in mind. I have all the responsibilities of parenting when the kids are with us, yet many of the traditional joys of being a mother I will never know. I will never be able to recount to my children the stories of their births. They will never have my eyes or my DNA.

But what they do have is my heart. They have stolen that in spades. So I settle for a new picture taken with an eternal lens. A perspective that says I may live in a fractured, broken world, and my life may look nothing like I thought it would, but God will reframe that for me if I allow him to. For he and he alone can redeem and reshape my disappointed heart.

Boasting in Our Brokenness

I love how Paul ultimately responded to God's no. Once he understood that God's grace was sufficient and God's strength would be shown in weakness, he wrote, "Therefore most gladly I will rather boast in my infirmities, that the power of Christ may rest upon me" (2 Corinthians 12:9).

Paul didn't shut down his heart in disappointment. He didn't crawl under the covers and wish the world away. He didn't waste opportunities to be present in his life just because it was turning out differently from the way he had pictured it. Instead he surrendered. He handed over his preconceived notions and gave God free rein. He was basically saying, "Okay, God, if this is the story, if this is how you are going to write it, then let's get the most out of it. I'm not just going to live with my infirmities; I'm going to boast in them. It's worth it if your power will be shown in my life."

And it was. In fact, we are still reading about God's power in Paul's life today.

Your life and mine hold the same potential. The power of God will be seen through us as we boldly share our broken places so that other disappointed hearts can be healed.

CHAPTER SIX

THE CONTROLLING HEART

There are only two kinds of people in the end: those who
say to God, "Thy will be done," and those to whom
God says, in the end, "Thy will be done."

C. S. LEWIS

CONTROL ISSUES can be difficult to discern because they take so many forms. Some controllers are pushy and abusive, but others seem nice and well-meaning. Some are sneaky and subtle. And some have no awareness of how manipulative they are.

The urge to control can manifest itself in many different ways—some obvious, some more subtle. It can be seen in

- the hovering mother who won't let her children breathe without telling them when and where;
- the friend who doles out unwanted advice "for your own good";
- the husband who won't let his wife out of his sight or enslaves her with his emotional or physical abuse;
- the in-law who forgot the "leave and cleave" part of an adult child's marriage vows;

- the business owner who won't delegate responsibility because "no one will do it as well as I can";
- the employee who won't take a lunch break because the office will "fall apart";
- the wife who treats her husband like a child instead of a spouse; or
- the pastor who refuses to be questioned.

Any of these people sound familiar? Most of us have been victims of people with control issues from time to time. And I suspect that most of us have been controllers as well, though we may not recognize it in ourselves.

As I began to study this issue of control, I discovered it is often closely related to other issues of the heart. For instance, a controlling heart often creates a performing one: one person's attempts at control produce performances from those around him. Or people who have suffered serious disappointment can develop controlling tendencies in reaction to the pain. Criticism and weariness (explored in later chapters) can have control components, and a controlling heart can also develop out of insecurity or pride.

The energy behind controlling behavior, however, almost always comes from one of two emotions: anger or fear. Perhaps they have been betrayed by a husband or wife, so they're determined to keep the errant spouse under their thumb. (That's anger.) Or maybe they were hurt and want to make sure they are never hurt that way again. (That's fear.) They may feel passed over, so they will try to keep other people from reaching their fullest potential (anger again).

Whatever the emotional impetus, all controlling hearts share a central motivation: *They're all about self.* There is no sugar-coating this reality. The controlling heart seeks self-preservation or self-satisfaction or self-exaltation—*self* all the way. And there is no love in it. A heart that shuts down because of control issues also shuts down love.

You may think that's a harsh statement. It seems harsh to me too—especially when I am honest about my own controlling tendencies. But the Bible makes it clear that love and self-seeking are complete opposites. Or as the Amplified Bible puts it, "Love (God's love in us) does not insist on its own rights or its own way" (1 Corinthians 13:5). And control is essentially a matter of seeking our own way over everything else.

Of all the shut-down hearts, I sincerely believe this one is the most dangerous—both for the controllers and for those they try to control.

Power Plays and Masked Manipulation

The controlling heart, as I've indicated, can reveal itself in a variety of tactics and employ a number of different tools. The specific ways a person seeks to control depend partly on personality and temperament (extroverted or introverted, bold or shy), partly on life experience (what has worked before and what hasn't worked), and partly on circumstances (what will work in a given situation). But the goal is always the same—to make sure the controllers get what they want or think they need.

The most obvious tactic a controller uses is what I call the "power play"—a barefaced bid to get his or her own way. Those who use this approach simply want what they want, and they'll push hard until they get it (or until somebody stops them). Power players can be mean, bullying, or intimidating, using anger or even threats to get what they want.

Even when they're not overtly abusive, power players tend to be direct and demanding. They demand that others come on board with what they want, and if thwarted, they will either push harder or cut the other person off. Power players do not keep people in their lives who disagree with them. Instead, they simply surround themselves with people who tell them what they want to hear. If there is a person who speaks truth into their lives, they will find every possible reason to discount that truth.

Do any of us like to hear someone tell us we might be wrong? No. We come out of the womb wanting to know we're right. If we have any kind of healthy perspective about ourselves, we know we're going to be wrong from time to time. In fact, we'll probably be wrong far more than we are right. We understand that our real friends are the ones who are honest with us, even if their honesty hurts. But power players don't see things that way. They would rather discard those who get in the way of what they desire.

Bribery and punishment are also common tactics of power players. They promise something of value to convince another person to comply with their wishes, or they may withhold something as punishment for a person who doesn't comply. Money, privileges, or information can be used to secure control—the only requirement is that it matters to the person being controlled. For example, a controlling spouse may withhold sex as punishment or use the promise of sex to control a partner instead of enjoying it as the gift it's supposed to be.

A variation on the punishment tactic is the silent treatment: "I will punish you by not speaking to you." I have to admit that I was once a master at this. I could be silent for days. I desperately wanted to get my first husband to acknowledge my pain, but withdrawing was all I knew how to do. Instead of verbalizing how I felt, which I was far too fearful to do because of some past experiences, I would just go quiet. But the silent treatment never accomplished what I was after. I longed for lasting change. All I got, though, was just another reminder of how broken I really was.

Actually, the silent treatment contains elements of a second general approach to control, one I call "masked manipulation." This approach to control is far more subtle—and way sneakier—than the power play. Masked manipulators still want their own way and will do almost anything to get it. Instead of approaching the situation head-on, they use more indirect forms of persuasion and often cover them with fake agreement, sweetness, and smiles.

The masked manipulation version of demanding, for instance, would be the pointed suggestion. It might sound perfectly innocent—"Don't you think you should do this?" or "Wouldn't it be better if we did that?"—but the underlying meaning is "I want you to do this or that." This type of control is so sneaky. The controller will try to make others think the suggestion was their own idea, when they are really being baited and manipulated.

Spouses tend to be great at manipulative suggestions. So do children. And so do Southerners, who have been taught, above all, to act sweet and polite. But the goal of masked manipulation is anything but sweet. It is simply an indirect form of demanding our own way.

Flattery is another form of masked manipulation. This strategy for controlling others is learned early, when kids move past the "no" stage and realize that being obstinate isn't a real motivator for adults. When my niece Georgia looks at me and says, "You're the best Aunt Niecy ever," she knows I would move the world for her. And believe me, she uses that.

So do our own kids. I often hear, "Niecy, do you know you're the best bonus mom ever?"

My response is always, "Yes, actually I do." That kind of stops them in their tracks.

The use of flattery and sweet talk as a control tactic is not limited to kids, of course. I've watched people flatter their way to the top of their fields without any talent to back them up. I've sat in meetings with people who have told me all kinds of wonderful things about my books and Bible studies, only to discern that they wanted something from me. I love sweet people. I do. I gravitate to them. I hope people find me sweet. But when flattery is used as a tool for manipulation or control, it doesn't feel sweet at all.

Perhaps the most maddening form of masked manipulation is what is often called "passive aggression." People who are afraid to speak their own minds or expose their true feelings sometimes resort to this kind of control tactic. Passive aggressive people make promises but then "forget" to keep them. They agree to do something, yet it never gets accomplished. They say yes, but only to get the other person off their backs or out of their way. And then they do exactly as they please.

A particularly painful form of control involves using guilt to control others. Controllers who know about the stuff in another person's past love to wield that knowledge as a weapon. They bring up all the ways the other person has failed—especially failed them personally—because they know fear of exposure, shame, and honest regret can keep the "guilty party" in submission to their whims and wishes.

A related form of manipulation is playing the victim. Controllers who take this tack use their own life stories—or carefully selected versions of them—to play on the sympathies of others. They make it clear (and often believe) that everyone is against them, that life has never worked out for them. That because they have been through so much, surely they deserve to get what they want.

Negotiating and bargaining—the old "I'll give you this if you'll give me that"—can be yet another form of masked manipulation. Have you ever been in a relationship with someone who gives you nothing unless you give him or her something in return? Real love doesn't work that way; it gives without expecting to be loved back. But manipulators demand everything while convincing you that you have just gotten a great deal.

I could go on and on here with all the different tactics this deceptively sinful form of a shut-down heart can use. But what is most important to realize is that the controlling heart—whether openly demanding or sneakily manipulative—is the very opposite of what it claims to be—in control.

The Origins of the Controlling Heart

Power plays, masked manipulation, and other manifestations of the controlling heart are nothing new, of course. The Bible is full of examples, beginning in the Garden.

The Genesis story tells us, "The serpent was the shrewdest of all the wild animals the LORD God had made (3:1, NLT). The King James Version uses the word *subtil* (an older form of *subtle*). Another possible translation is *cunning*. All these terms imply the desire and ability to control or manipulate others.[1] This is where it all began—in the Garden. In the very beginning.

Look who started it: the serpent—that is, Satan, the embodiment of evil.

And look what it tapped into: "When the woman saw that the tree was good for food, and that it was pleasant to the eyes, and a tree to be desired to make one wise, she took of the fruit thereof, and did eat, and gave also unto her husband with her; and he did eat" (Genesis 3:6, KJV).

What did Satan's manipulation appeal to in Eve? Here's a hint: the word translated *desired* in the King James Version implies "lust."[2] Satan's "suggestion" ultimately appealed to Eve's lust, her intense craving to acquire something for herself.

Look at the other descriptions here: "good for food," "pleasant to the eyes," "to be desired to make one wise." Does this sound familiar at all? If not, here's a hint from the New Testament: "For everything in the world—the lust of the flesh, the lust of the eyes, and the pride of life—comes not from the Father but from the world" (1 John 2:16, NIV).

The enemy goes after our human, fleshly desire for self. He manipulated Eve's heart by targeting her sense of self. And it worked because, as Max Lucado writes, "We humans want to do things our way. Forget the easy way. Forget the common way. Forget the best way. Forget God's way. We want to do things *our* way."[3]

Look at what Eve's selfish lust, her insistence on "my way" eventually got her. Everything she truly desired was stripped away. Why? Because her motive for having it was so impure. It was all about her. And as a result of her actions, God moved her and that man of hers right out of the Garden. Eve tried to have it all, and she ended up losing everything she had—along with her sweet face-to-face fellowship with her Father.

That's one of the many dangers of a controlling heart. Often the one thing you are so desperate to control ends up being exactly what you lose. My friend, be very careful. The person or circumstance you are so desperate to hang on to might very well end up being the one thing that slips through your fingers. That child. That marriage. That career.

And of course it goes without saying that letting control issues shut down your heart is a sin.

The Lie of the Controlling Heart: "God Isn't Big Enough"

What is the lie that creates the controlling heart, that triggers the anger and fear beneath our power plays and masked manipulations? The lie of the controlling heart is that *God isn't big enough,* that he can't be trusted to run the world the right way or to take care of us. That God isn't in control, so we have to be.

The enemy of our hearts is always fighting hard to try to put God on a human level and us on a godlike level. Isn't that what he did to Adam and Eve in the Garden? Remember what he said when Eve related what God had told her about the forbidden tree?

"'You won't die!' the serpent replied to the woman. 'God knows that your eyes will be opened as soon as you eat [the fruit], and you will be like God, knowing both good and evil'" (Genesis 3:4-5, NLT).

In other words, "No, really, Eve. God is just petty. He thinks like you think. He doesn't want you to have this because he doesn't want you to be like him." The serpent was ascribing human motivations and behavior to God. And if the devil can convince us at any time that God is like us—petty, judgmental, envious—there is no way we will believe that God can be trusted to keep the world spinning and to handle the situations of our lives.

But oh, our hearts are desperate to know that God is bigger than we are, that he is in control of the universe and can handle our lives too. Who wants a God just like us anyway? No one. Yet when we believe this lie, we convince ourselves that we are the only grown-ups in the room and that it's up to us to make sure the world goes around.

One of the most awesome displays of God's bigness is found in the book of Job. Basically, this amazing passage gives God's responses to Job's questions and challenges. It's a long passage, but I want to quote a taste of it here.

"Where were you when I laid the foundations
of the earth?

Tell me, if you know so much.
Who determined its dimensions
    and stretched out the surveying line?
What supports its foundations,
    and who laid its cornerstone
as the morning stars sang together
    and all the angels shouted for joy?

"Who kept the sea inside its boundaries
    as it burst from the womb,
and as I clothed it with clouds
    and wrapped it in thick darkness?
For I locked it behind barred gates,
    limiting its shores.
I said, 'This far and no farther will you come.
    Here your proud waves must stop!'

"Have you ever commanded the morning to appear
    and caused the dawn to rise in the east?
Have you made daylight spread to the ends of the earth,
    to bring an end to the night's wickedness?
As the light approaches,
    the earth takes shape like clay pressed beneath a seal;
    it is robed in brilliant colors.
The light disturbs the wicked
    and stops the arm that is raised in violence.

"Have you explored the springs from which the
    seas come?
    Have you explored their depths?
Do you know where the gates of death are located?
    Have you seen the gates of utter gloom?

Do you realize the extent of the earth?
Tell me about it if you know!"
JOB 38:4-18, NLT

Wow! The power and bigness of God have never been more beautifully stated, more clearly defined. The next time we stare at the ocean that stops at the tips of our toes, the next time we take in that early morning dawn, may we be reminded of the undeniable greatness of our God. *Our God.*

The God who holds us and cares for us and can handle any situation we may ever face or dream of facing. The God who changes our lives when we give up our desperate, fearful, angry quest for control and choose his way instead.

Reclaiming the Controlling Heart

As with the other hearts we've looked at, reclaiming the controlling heart begins with recognizing that control is an issue for us. And that's not always easy. It's usually easy to recognize controlling behavior in other people—especially when they're trying to control us! But recognizing our own control issues can be tricky.

If you suspect that one of the behaviors you read about earlier in this chapter might be something you do, then owning that is where this begins.

How do you know? If you've ever had a friend, acquaintance, or even an enemy accuse you of having "control issues," it may be time to listen—especially if more than one friend, acquaintance, or enemy has brought it up. Even if everything in you is protesting and you're absolutely sure this isn't a problem for you, it couldn't hurt to dig a little deeper.

Here's another hint that control may be an issue: you're easily frustrated when dealing with people, and you often find yourself weary and frantic. If your life and your relationships feel out of control, part of the problem may be your own controlling heart.

I suggest you begin by asking God if this is true of you. He will reveal the truth to you if you seek it. You might also ask a friend whom you trust to tell you. If you have surrounded yourself with people who only tell you what you want to hear, find a godly counselor and ask him or her. If you truly want to avoid the perils of a controlling heart, you will leave no stone unturned.

Keep in mind that you don't have to be a complete control freak to struggle with these issues. We all struggle with a tendency to control at times. We are all prone to self-centered behavior and manipulation. But what you're looking for are patterns of behavior, things you do over and over again.

Jesus told his disciples:

> "Anyone who intends to come with me has to let me
> lead. You're not in the driver's seat; I am. Don't run
> from suffering; embrace it. Follow me and I'll show
> you how. Self-help is no help at all. Self-sacrifice is the
> way, my way, to finding yourself, your true self. What
> kind of deal is it to get everything you want but lose
> yourself? What could you ever trade your soul for?"
> MATTHEW 16:24-26, *The Message*

The key to reclaiming a controlling heart, a truth we should reflect on time and time again, is this: we have to relinquish the driver's seat to God. And let's be honest—that's not easy for people with control issues. If your heart is extremely shut down in this way, voluntarily giving up your power may be the hardest thing you have ever done. But if you cannot manage to hand over the wheel and trust God to run your life and the universe, you'll be setting yourself up for the ultimate loss.

Alive and Free

Reclaiming the controlling heart begins with doing our best to recognize our behavioral patterns and motivations. It continues with consciously relinquishing the wheel of our lives to our big, trustworthy God—and then, if necessary, doing it over and over. Again, it's not easy. It's a process, not a one-time transformation. But as we persist in doing this, our rigid, stubborn, shut-down, and controlling hearts will begin to soften into open, alive ones. And as that happens, we'll gradually see our controlling behaviors—demands and "suggestions," intimidation and flattery, guilt, victimization, bargaining, and passive aggression—subside. We'll begin to operate out of our alive hearts.

How does an alive heart differ from one shut down by the urge to control?

The main difference, as I see it, is freedom.

Instead of being bent on controlling others or being hurt because others are trying to control us, when we live out of our alive hearts we make friends with freedom. Interestingly enough, this profoundly healing process doesn't just liberate us from our own controlling tendencies. It also reduces the ability of other people to control us.

As we learn to live out of our alive hearts, we grow more comfortable in granting others the freedom to think and feel without coercing or manipulating them. We're all right with their having opinions and expressing them, even if those opinions are painful to us. Instead of demanding compliance or (strongly) suggesting what needs to happen, we'll ask, "What do you think?"—and actually listen!

An alive heart doesn't have to keep score. It doesn't operate tit for tat: "If you do this, then I get to do that. If you win this battle, be sure I'll win the next one." An alive heart knows there will be moments in life when you need more than I need and seasons when I need more than you do. And real love is okay with that.

If we're living out of alive hearts, we'll accept the fact that we don't have to bully or flatter people to get them on our side—because we're simply okay if not everyone agrees with us. In fact, we can get to a place of such freedom that we can even grant others the freedom not to love us the way we prefer to be loved—because we can trust our big, loving God to provide us with what we need. Once we get our minds and hearts around that indisputable fact, the need to bargain with others and manipulate them to get what we want will diminish.

One of the most exciting things I've discovered about living out of an alive heart is that I can simply talk about what I want and need instead of using manipulation to get it. Because of the particular shape of my own shut-down heart, learning to do this has been a revelation for me.

Philly and I learned a new saying in our sessions with our counselor, Ken, and we use it often these days: "Assume freedom." I've come to see this as the essence of the way an alive heart responds to life. Instead of worrying about what others might think or how they might respond to me, I can simply assume that I'm free to express myself and leave the reaction of the other person up to him or her.

I've always been something of a pouter. When I encountered conflict, I tended to just shut down verbally, and the pain of my first marriage made that behavior far worse. But gradually, with Philly's help and the "assume freedom" idea firmly in mind, I began to move past this habitual shut-down response. One memorable early morning, I reached a turning point. Good for me. Not so good for Philly.

Philly and I had both been single for a while by the time we married, so adjusting to each other's sleeping habits was a bit of a shock for both of us. I liked complete silence. He needed a box fan for white noise. I would wrap myself around a pillow because I needed to be touching something all night. He couldn't stand to be touched. I liked my covers all scrunched up around my neck, and he liked the blankets neatly folded and straight. I'm talking complete opposites. And our differences in this area led to natural misunderstandings.

In my case, these were made worse by some lingering wounds from my past. I had lived with a lot of rules in my first marriage—rules that dictated what I could and couldn't do in our relationship. I never liked those rules, but in my shut-down state I had acquiesced to them. Even long after my divorce, my hurt over those rules still lingered. I didn't even know that hurt was there until I was in another intimate relationship.

One morning Philly slammed up against all that pain I was still carrying inside. His personal sleeping quirks didn't even approach the extreme of what I'd experienced in my previous marriage, but on this day they pushed all my buttons. I lay in bed perfectly still, silent and seething, the anger and hurt and fear racing through me like a hamster going full throttle in his wheel.

Then I stopped and thought about what I was doing. And I decided that my old shut-down heart could not have me anymore. I had to respond to this moment differently from the way I had responded in the past.

What did I do? I assumed freedom. I got out of the bed, so agitated that I needed to pace. And I said, in a very loud and exasperated voice, "You just have so many rules. I lived with rules for too many years, and I won't live like that again! I'm not living with all these—these *rules!*"

I'm not saying that yelling at Philly early in the morning was the best way to deal with the situation. Our moments of friction are usually handled much more calmly than this one was. Yet for me in that moment, this was a major breakthrough. That I was saying anything at all was huge! And that I was coming to my heart's defense was monumental.

I was almost like Giselle in the movie *Enchanted* when she says, "You make me so . . . so . . . angry!"[4] Then she throws her hands over her mouth and starts laughing because anger is such a new emotion for her. For me, that moment was just as new and healing.

My sweet husband was so gracious with my heart. Philly understood that my outburst wasn't necessarily about him but about my own broken places. The step I took that day to express what mattered to me and the way he handled my heart have led both of us to a new place of freedom with each other and in our own journeys.

The Power of Peace

Another important—and healing—aspect of living with an alive heart comes as a direct result of trusting our big, capable God with our past hurts and failures. Instead of holding our grudges or deep wounds close or, even worse, holding them over someone else's head, we learn to let them go and make peace with both our past and our present. This almost always involves forgiving others and ourselves, seeking forgiveness from those we've hurt, and then deliberately choosing to let go of our resentments. Not necessarily "forgive and forget," but leaving those hurts and failures in God's hands and refusing to let them control us. Again, this will be a process, not a one-time choice. But it is amazing how making peace with the past reduces our own controlling tendencies and also protects us from the pain of others' control tactics. It's hard to lay a guilt trip, for instance, on a person who has already dealt with his or her guilt.

See, friend, peace is not the absence of opposition, as a controlling heart would have us believe. Real peace is the confident, nonfrantic trust that David talked about in Psalm 131:2—"Surely I have calmed and quieted my soul, like a weaned child with his mother; like a weaned child is my soul within me."

It's the peace of a person with a reclaimed heart who truly understands how big and dependable God is.

We will never be able to control what people think about us. We will never be able to control other people's actions toward us. We will never be able to control how life will turn out for us.

Sure, we may manipulate these things for a season, but the effect won't be lasting. So why wear ourselves out trying? Why not realize that our God is big enough to take care of everything that concerns us. Why not rest ourselves on his breast and enjoy what his love and protection afford us—sleep, peaceful sleep, with God, and God only, in control.

CHAPTER SEVEN

THE CRITICAL HEART

Criticism of others is . . . an oblique form of self-commendation.
We think we make the picture hang straight on our wall by
telling our neighbors that all his pictures are crooked.
FULTON J. SHEEN

IT HAPPENED on a Sunday, the one day of the week when everyone should be kind, patient, loving—you know, display all those attitudes that might not come as easy the other days of the week. Philly and I had just left the church parking lot when the criticism started. I began with one person and went to the next and then to the next, listing one fault and offense after another. Then, about halfway through the fourth person, I heard myself and stopped.

I turned to my husband. Smart man that he is, he kept his eyes glued to the road and said nothing. So I said it for him. "Wow, babe, there's a lot up in there."

He nodded. "I'm thinking there is."

We've all done our share of criticizing, of course—griping, judging, accusing, blaming, faultfinding, sniping and throwing

119

zingers, badmouthing others. We get annoyed or irritated or just want to make ourselves look better, and we end up making pronouncements like

- ◆ "It's way too cold (or hot) in here. You'd think someone would know how to adjust a thermostat."
- ◆ "They let their kids run wild. Have they ever heard of discipline?"
- ◆ "Someone should have stopped her from going out in that color. It looks *awful* on her."
- ◆ "My wife is clueless half the time."
- ◆ "I wish my husband knew how to provide for his family like Sheila's husband provides for his."

I'm sure you get the point. On and on we go, with more critiques than Simon Cowell on a good day. Sometimes we utter them out loud. Sometimes we roll them over and over in our thoughts. And sometimes we criticize ourselves more strongly than we would ever criticize another person.

Not all criticism is harmful, of course. There are times when it's appropriate to share a negative opinion or make a judgment about what is wrong or right. Criticism really can be constructive. You'd know this if you ever sat at our dinner table. But let's be honest—often it's not constructive at all. In fact, it can be downright destructive when we let a critical spirit invade our hearts.

As with the other hearts, shutting down to the point where all we can see are the faults of others is usually a gradual process, though it can be triggered by a lot of different events.

Many of us came by our critical hearts honestly. We learned by example. We listened to our parents, our teachers, coaches, bosses, and the media dish out a steady stream of criticism.

And often—in the case of parents and teachers especially—it was directed at us.

Unfortunately it's a way of thinking that tends to be passed from generation to generation. Parents and teachers who were raised with this kind of criticism tend to pass it on—both out of their own woundedness and because they assume that's the way parenting and teaching are done. That's why it is important, if you were raised by someone with a critical heart, that you pay even greater attention to how you engage the hearts of your own children or students.

A critical heart can also be a by-product of disappointment and can coexist with other hearts. Disappointed hearts can easily become angry, isolated, or viciously critical. When someone has repeatedly broken our trust, when we've been perpetually overlooked for that job we wanted, or when we've been let down by people who should have had our backs, disappointment is a natural response. And when we refuse to deal with that disappointment by releasing it to our Father through honest prayer, praise, and singing, the disappointment can reveal itself in a critical spirit.

And though these criticisms are mostly targeted at the person we are disappointed with, that isn't always the case. An innocent party close at hand might just become an easy target for our frustration. Or sometimes, when we do criticize the person who let us down, the criticism may bear little relation to the offense.

As the words pour out of our broken, wounded souls, they hurt those we're criticizing but also reflect the true state of our hearts—because every time we open our mouths, we choose what will come out. Proverbs 18:21 states it succinctly: "Words kill, words give life; they're either poison or fruit—you choose" (*The Message*).

The Pitfalls of Legalism

The 2004 movie *Saved!*, which is about students at a Christian school, includes a scene where a Christian "mean girl" literally throws a Bible at another girl and shouts, "I am *filled* with Christ's love. You are just jealous of my success in the Lord."

The girl she hits simply picks up the Bible and hands it back to her with the words "This is not a weapon."[1]

I find so much sad truth in that little scene. For too many of us, church has been the very weapon that caused us to shut down our hearts. It is where we have been judged the most, criticized the most, or encountered the majority of our wounds. It is also where we might have seen the critical spirit modeled and developed a critical spirit of our own.

It's been happening since the time of the Pharisees. People who are hungry for God come up against a version of religion that focuses most on what they do or what they look like and binds them with a collection of rules instead of freeing them to live out of their hearts. This misguided view relegates the beauty of a relationship with God to nothing but a set of regulations, leaving people lost in a maze of negativism and criticism.

In Jesus' day, the Pharisees got bent out of shape over topics like associating with tax collectors or picking grain on the Sabbath. In my parents' and grandparents' era, it was about playing cards or wearing makeup or going to the movies. In ours, it might be more about serving on certain committees or adopting the "appropriate" political stance. The specifics change, but the spirit remains the same. When this is how we are raised, in a culture that obsesses about dos and don'ts, it's easy to fall into the trap of hard-line, get-it-right religion that criticizes anyone who doesn't follow the rules.

Having grown up in a legalistic denomination that has taken huge strides in recent years to move from a "works" mind-set to a more heart-centered one, I do have a certain sympathy for these hard-line folks. Why? Because I've been where they are. But as I've tried to work through my own legalistic issues and the damage that some of my upbringing did to my heart, I've found a new revelation in what Paul wrote in Romans 14.

> Who are you to judge someone else's servants? Whether they are faithful or not is their own master's concern. They will be faithful, because the Lord has the power to make them faithful.
>   Some people consider one day to be more holy than another. Others think all days are the same. Each person should be absolutely sure in his own mind. Those who think one day is special do it to honor the Lord. Those who eat meat do it to honor the Lord. They give thanks to God. Those who don't eat meat do it to honor the Lord. They also give thanks to God.
> vv. 4-6, NIrV

Prejudicial Criticism

Many of us criticize out of our prejudices—judging those who don't look like us, act like us, believe like us, talk like us, or worship like us. The term *prejudice* is often used for racist attitudes—and believe me, there's still plenty of racial prejudice around. But prejudice rears its head whenever we encounter someone different from us and make judgments out of our preconceptions about what "they" are like.

Do you know what life and time have taught me? The fact that another person doesn't do something the way I do doesn't mean that person is wrong. It certainly doesn't mean all the judgments I might make about what "they"—the other person's group—are like will be true. And it definitely doesn't give me the right to let loose with my criticism.

My parents are a real demonstration of how two very different people can accept one another without criticism. I was raised in the Pentecostal tradition. But even within those parameters, my parents' worship styles are quite different from each other. My father is a demonstrative worshiper. My mother worships quietly. My father is loud and crazy at times. My mother is demure and always a lady. I've heard my father pray in his prayer language on numerous occasions. I've heard my mother do this only three times.

Are my parents different? Yes. Could people try to measure their relationship with God based on the outward ways in which they worship? I'm sure some do. Some may think my dad is more spiritual because he is more charismatic. Others may think my mother is more spiritual because she is more reserved.

But that is why God is so amazing. He looks at their hearts. He sees them both as broken individuals whom he loves—and who love him. And I believe he rejoices in both of their styles of worship.

The other day, my mother mentioned another pastor's wife she had met, a woman who was very involved at their church. I heard her tell my father, "I probably wasn't that good of a pastor's wife."

He answered gently, "You were exactly the pastor's wife you were meant to be." And anyone who knows her would agree.

We would do well to take that spirit and apply it to the many circumstances where we meet people who are different from us. If we simply open our hearts and our eyes, we'll learn that we're not so different after all . . . or that our differences don't matter much in the end . . . or that even in cases of significant differences, there are plenty of constructive ways to bridge the gap between us. Criticism based on prejudice rarely builds bridges, but it does destroy hearts.

Jesus dealt with a lot of prejudice in his day, but there was probably no greater prejudicial divide than between the Jews and the Gentiles. When Paul later began evangelizing the Greeks—definitely Gentiles—his fellow Jews, who had grown up believing that Gentiles were inferior, were in an uproar. But this is what he told them: "There is no distinction between Jew and Greek. The same Lord is Lord over all [of us] and He generously bestows His riches upon all who call upon Him [in faith]" (Romans 10:12, AMP).

Then Paul went on to explain this to his Gentile followers, who apparently had some of their own ideas about the Jews as well. He compared the Jews to an olive tree and the Gentiles to a branch of the tree that had been grafted in. He said:

> If some of the branches were broken off, while you, a wild olive shoot, were grafted in among them to share the richness [of the root and sap] of the olive tree, do not boast over the branches and pride yourself at their expense. If you do boast and feel superior, remember it is not you that support the root, but the root [that supports] you.
> ROMANS 11:17-18, AMP

I'm not Jewish. In fact, to be honest, I don't know a lot of Jewish people. So what I hear in this passage is that having this gospel at all is a gift, a privilege! The fact that Jesus would come to save everyone, not just his own people, is more than we could ask for. It had very little to do with us or what group we happen to belong to. But it had everything to do with who he is.

I'm pretty sure that when we get to heaven, we'll find that

Jesus isn't a Baptist or a Pentecostal. We'll discover that Jesus isn't a Republican or a Democrat. (Some of you just fell out of your chairs!) He probably won't look like those pictures that hung on the walls of your Sunday school room.

No, what I suspect we'll learn is that Jesus simply loves us—all of us. And boy, does he do that well. He does it without prejudice or preconception.

What a gift if we could learn to do that too.

The Birth of Blaming

This critical spirit has been with us from the very beginning. Or at least it showed up right after the Fall. Adam and Eve disobeyed God, ate of the fruit, and discovered they were naked. And then, as they were sewing together their fig leaves, they heard God coming.

> Then the LORD God called to the man, "Where are you?"
>
> He replied, "I heard you walking in the garden, so I hid. I was afraid because I was naked."
>
> "Who told you that you were naked?" the LORD God asked. "Have you eaten from the tree whose fruit I commanded you not to eat?"
>
> The man replied, "It was the woman you gave me who gave me the fruit, and I ate it."
> GENESIS 3:9-12, NLT

Do you notice that? The instant Adam heard God calling, he knew he had done the wrong thing, and he couldn't stand being in the wrong. So he used this opportunity to deflect the blame, first on Eve and then on God himself, all in an effort to make himself look like the victim instead of the perpetrator.

No, he didn't actively criticize Eve in the moment, but the critical spirit was there, and I have no doubt the criticism followed. Because Adam was already well on his way to developing a critical heart. His actions exposed his determination to be in the right and to make sure others knew they were in the wrong.

Sadly, we've been doing that ever since.

The Lie of the Critical Heart: "God Expects Me to Get It Right"

So what is the lie of the critical heart?

The lie is that *God expects us to be perfect, and his biggest concern is that we follow the rules to the letter and get everything right.*

It is understandable that this lie is a stronghold for many because it's based on an element of truth. Our God is indeed a righteous God, and he did give us rules to live by. The law of Moses, given in the early days of Israel and then built on by generations of God's people, absolutely required us to get it right, and if we didn't, the law laid out a *right* way to atone for our wrongness.

Having the law was definitely better than the lawlessness that had prevailed earlier. But what a weight it became to live under, especially when generation after generation of scribes started working on it and shaping it into the imposing system of regulations that people were expected to follow in Jesus' day. God knew it was a weight, which is one reason Jesus came. To remove us from the performance mind-set the law produced and to land us smack-dab in the middle of God's wide net of grace.

The group Phillips, Craig & Dean has a song called "Mercy Came Running." I especially appreciate this song because of its powerful personification of mercy. It talks about how, in the days before Jesus, priests would go into the Temple to make the sacrifice in the Holy of Holies and "mercy's face" would be "pressed against the veil." Hearing that song, you can practically see mercy just longing to break through the constraints of the law. As the title bears witness, Jesus' death finally accomplished that. When he died and then rose, mercy indeed came running. And it hasn't stopped.

But the enemy is so good at feeding the lie to us that the requirements of the law are still in place—and we're getting it all wrong. How easily he succeeds in getting us to accuse ourselves and others.

I've done this so many times. I have been so hard on myself and so hard on others, all because I swallowed this perverted lie that being right—doing right, thinking right, acting right—is the way to stay in God's good graces, as if we could ever be righteous enough for him.

But what about the Garden? Didn't Adam and Eve face consequences for their sin? Of course they did. Sin always brings consequences. But the story is deeper than that. What really caused Adam and Eve's downfall was what happened in their hearts. They allowed themselves to be turned from that sweet place of face-to-face intimacy with their Father toward the lies of the serpent. This fostered their distrust in God and eventually had them running away from the heart of the One who knew them best.

Yes, God made rules to protect the hearts of his children. But it was Satan who got them so focused on the rules themselves—what was right and wrong and fair and unfair— that they neglected the reason behind the rules—their relationship with God. And *that* was ultimately what got them thrown out of the Garden.

Jesus confronted the same perverted thinking in the

Pharisees, who loved rules. Rules gave the Pharisees a measure
for righteousness, a way of judging who was right and who was
wrong, and a basis for declaring themselves right and others
wrong. But then Jesus came and threw their entire system out
the window. As the apostle Paul put it:

> For what the law could not do in that it was weak
> through the flesh, God did by sending His own Son
> in the likeness of sinful flesh, on account of sin:
> He condemned sin in the flesh, that the righteous
> requirement of the law might be fulfilled in us who
> do not walk according to the flesh but according to
> the Spirit.
> ROMANS 8:3-4

What? No rules? Oh yes, there were still rules, but they
weren't the kind of rules the Pharisees were worrying about. The
apostle Paul explained this difference in the book of Romans,
addressing the controversy about whether new converts should
be circumcised like Jews. This issue pinpointed just how radi-
cally Jesus had overturned the Pharisees' assumptions. They had
based their entire sense of being right on following an elaborate
set of dos and don'ts. But obeying them was about something
else now. It was about the heart:

> For he is not a Jew who is one outwardly, nor is
> circumcision that which is outward in the flesh; but
> he is a Jew who is one inwardly; and circumcision is
> that of the heart, in the Spirit, not in the letter; whose
> praise is not from men but from God.
> ROMANS 2:28-29

In other words, the letter of the law, the Pharisees' focus, provides what humans can see. But Jesus' teachings focused on the intent *behind* the law—on the heart, which is seen by God alone. Remember what he said when asked about which commandment was greatest?

> "You must love the LORD your God with all your heart, all your soul, and all your mind." This is the first and greatest commandment. A second is equally important: "Love your neighbor as yourself." The entire law and all the demands of the prophets are based on these two commandments.
>
> MATTHEW 22:37-40, NLT

By boiling down the entire law to two commandments, Jesus was making things both easier and harder. Sure, two rules are easier to learn and remember than the elaborate code the Pharisees followed. But if we actually get serious about following these two great commandments, we'll see they're far more challenging. Why? Because they require us to encounter our hearts. They might actually reveal to us things about our hearts that need to change or be reclaimed.

If we have an external set of rules, if we think we know exactly what we're supposed to be doing, we don't really need to worry about what's inside us. All we have to do is keep our behavior right—or pretend to keep our behavior right. And if we have a clearly defined set of rules that lets us think we're getting it right, then they also provide us a measuring stick to know where others get it wrong.

You can see why the Pharisees were so disturbed by Jesus, can't you? Jesus overturned their entire belief system, their basis for feeling all right about God and about themselves. They really thought the rules were the heart of their religion. They believed it had been that way since the beginning.

But that wasn't true—not entirely. Yes, God gave the law. But he had also been trying to teach his people for centuries that his *primary* focus was on the heart. Psalm 51:16-17 (AMP), for instance, says this:

> For You delight not in sacrifice, or else would I give it; You find no pleasure in burnt offering.
>
> My sacrifice [the sacrifice acceptable] to God is a broken spirit; a broken and a contrite heart [broken down with sorrow for sin and humbly and thoroughly penitent], such, O God, You will not despise.

King David had this advice for his son Solomon:

> Know the God of your father, and serve Him with a loyal heart and with a willing mind; for the LORD searches all hearts and understands all the intent of the thoughts. If you seek Him, He will be found by you; but if you forsake Him, He will cast you off forever.
> 1 CHRONICLES 28:9

But despite the ongoing emphasis on the heart in the Old Testament, the coming of Jesus still changed things dramatically. What Jesus taught and what he did on the cross did not mark the beginning of God's interest in our hearts, but it did change what God sees when he looks at our hearts. When we have surrendered our hearts to Jesus, that is what God sees. He looks in our hearts and sees Jesus. And oh, how freeing it is to realize that.

In Galatians 5, where Paul spells out the fruit of the Spirit, all the "fruit" he mentions are heart qualities: "love, joy, peace, longsuffering, kindness, goodness, faithfulness, gentleness, self-control." Then, right after the list, Paul adds, "Against such there is no law" (Galatians 5:22-23).

When Jesus has our hearts, his fruit will ripen naturally in us, and we don't have to worry about all the dos and don'ts of the law. We won't have to obsess about the rules and getting them just right because our hearts will shift from a place of *need* to a place of *desire*: we will *want* to get it right. We'll want to serve him and help people who have less than we do. We'll long to pay tithes and give of our financial resources because we'll have learned that he is the provider of everything we have. We'll desire to love people well and be an example of Jesus wherever we go. And we'll make sure our words are life-giving because we'll know how easy it would be for others to point out the faults in our own lives.

That kind of heart . . . that is the heart God is after.

Reclaiming the Critical Heart

So how do we reclaim the critical heart? Once again, it starts with recognition, repentance, and reflecting on the truth of God's Word. And recognition begins with listening to ourselves, both our external conversation and our internal dialogue. How many of our words are complaining and judgmental, sarcastic or cutting? How many of our thoughts focus on what people are doing wrong?

Again, we're looking for patterns. One complaint about a waitress or a single gripe session with a friend does not necessarily indicate a critical heart. A habit of such remarks, though—especially if they're delivered with a lot of energy—might tell us something about ourselves. A critical or judgmental environment might be a clue as well, especially if we grew up with criticism.

It might even be helpful to ask others for an honest opinion: "Do you think I'm too negative, too hard on others or myself?"

If the answer is yes, now might be the time to rediscover grace, to become reacquainted with our amazingly generous and expansive God. Because once we understand at a heart level who he is and what he really wants from us, we'll find it a lot easier to leave the judgment to him.

Consider, for instance, the beautiful testimony of John the Baptist:

> John pointed [Jesus] out and called, "This is the One! The One I told you was coming after me but in fact was ahead of me. He has always been ahead of me, has always had the first word."

> We all live off his generous bounty,
>   gift after gift after gift.
> We got the basics from Moses,
>   and then this exuberant giving and receiving,
> This endless knowing and understanding—
>   all this came through Jesus, the Messiah.
> No one has ever seen God,
>   not so much as a glimpse.
> This one-of-a-kind God-Expression,
>   who exists at the very heart of the Father,
>   has made him plain as day.
> JOHN 1:15-18, *The Message*

The apostle John wrote later:

> This is how we know that we belong to the truth and how we set our hearts at rest in his presence: If our

hearts condemn us, we know that God is greater than our hearts, and he knows everything. Dear friends, if our hearts do not condemn us, we have confidence before God.

1 JOHN 3:19-21, NIV

I don't know about you, but that makes the Pentecostal girl in me want to dance! Even if my heart condemns me and criticizes others, God is still greater than my heart! I so need to know that because I lived for a long time with the very unhealthy perspective that I always had to get everything right. That there was no margin for my imperfections. And that if I didn't get everything right, then all of God's plans and purposes for me were thrown out the window. I cannot describe to you how I have tormented myself on more than one occasion with this distorted mind-set.

Friends, the pressure to live perfectly was never meant for us. Why else would Jesus say, "My grace is sufficient for you, for my power is made perfect in weakness" (2 Corinthians 12:9, NIV)? Why would the psalmist remind us, "The LORD is like a father to his children, tender and compassionate to those who fear him. For he knows how weak we are; he remembers we are only dust" (Psalm 103:13-14, NLT)?

Because he understands our imperfections, I suspect God isn't as rigid with us as we are with ourselves and others.

Does he long for us to do right?

Sure.

Does he long for us to desire his will for our lives?

Absolutely.

Does he call us to seek righteousness and examine our hearts?

Continually.

But does he require us to be perfect in the sense that we keep all the rules to the letter and never fail or make mistakes? I'm convinced he doesn't.

Aren't you grateful that God looks at your heart and not just at how "right" you are, how well you keep the rules?

He knows when our hearts want to do what is right and honor him, and he knows when they don't. He isn't looking for performance or perfection but for a heart that loves him. He can use that every time.

What Is My Job?

I've heard that Ruth Graham once said of her husband, "It's my job to love Billy; it's God's job to make him good." I haven't been able to track down the exact source of that quote, but I think its wisdom applies to those of us who are trying to reclaim a critical heart. Once we've gotten a good sense of God's grace toward us, we may need to make a point of allowing other people to live in the same grace.

Some of us have spent our lives thinking it is our job to point out other people's mistakes and alert the world when they aren't doing things the right way. But who appointed us to that position? How can we be sure we're right? How can we know all the variables? How can we even begin to measure another person's heart?

I'm pretty sure God doesn't measure sin the way we do. To illustrate this in my speaking engagements, I'll often stand on one side of the speaking platform. I talk about how we love to categorize and measure others' sins. We place ourselves at one point and position the person to whom we are comparing our-selves a little farther away. But then I walk clear across to the other side of the room and reveal that this is where God stands. The chasm between us and God is far greater than the tiny little distance between us and someone else's heart. And in light of how far we are from him, it's clear that our need for him is just as great as anyone else's.

I've learned that many people who find it easy to criticize others have often never truly admitted the reality of their own sin or the depth of their need for Jesus.

I lived this way for years, I'm horrified to say. I was a good girl. I never really did anything "bad." Oh, I did some silly things growing up—smoked some cigarettes (my granddaddy was a tobacco farmer), cheated on a test in high school (okay, two—and got caught both times), and tried a few beers. But I steered clear of anything major. I have always loved people well, served God with everything I had, loved him since I was little, and spent my life desiring to hear his heart for me. So when I encountered someone with "bigger" sin than mine, I felt pretty good about myself. I never actually said so, but I really did assume that Jesus probably only needed half a cross to save me.

Then came my divorce. As I walked through those painful days, the reality of what a sinner I am crashed in on me; I was brought face-to-face with the extent of my need for my Savior. I realized I needed him just as much as the prostitute selling her soul on the corner because I felt just as much shame. And oh, how that changed me.

I had judged divorced people for years. I had judged all kinds of people for years. Remember, I was raised in a religious tradition that spelled out the rules in black and white and made it clear that those who kept the rules to the letter were automatically better than those who broke them.

Then suddenly I was one of the rule breakers. And yes, I faced criticism and judgment. I criticized and judged myself. But I also encountered grace—amazing, astounding, life-changing grace. Grace from my heavenly Father and grace from so many people who love him and chose to love me. When you encounter that kind of grace, you will never be the same. Your heart will be moved with compassion in a way it never has been before.

Today, when I encounter people who habitually criticize, who try so desperately to convince themselves that *they* would never do what they are judging in others, who can't even speak without pointing out a fault in someone else, my heart breaks for them. Why? Because I know what it is like to live that way. I know the sin in it. And I know the beauty that comes when you get a glimpse of the depth and height and width of God's love, the lengths he went to save us "while we were still sinners" (Romans 5:8).

My own heart grew critical not only because of my upbringing but also because of my disappointment. Was my disappointment real? Yes, it was as real as a chicken is meant to be fried. But its being real didn't make my response right. Even now, when my heart still has to grieve some of the pain of my first marriage and its aftermath, I can feel myself wanting to get critical yet again. But Jesus lovingly and gently reminds me of how desperately I need him, and I try to release those who have wounded me into his care.

My God is big enough to handle the wrongs people do. My job is simply to depend on him and extend his love and grace to others as much as I can in recognition of my own sinfulness and gratitude for the love and grace he has extended to me in the midst of it.

"I Am"

Novelist and essayist G. K. Chesterton, whom C. S. Lewis considered his spiritual father, was once asked to comment on a big question: "What's wrong with the world?" A number of other thinkers were asked as well, but Chesterton's reply was the shortest and most to the point: "Dear Sirs: I am. Sincerely yours, G. K. Chesterton."[2]

John Stott, the British clergyman and a leader of the global evangelical movement, wrote something similar: "Before we can begin to see the cross as something done for us, we have to see it as something done by us."[3]

I believe that's key to reclaiming the critical heart. We need to get clear about our own sin and our ongoing inability to get it all right, but also about the reality of God's grace to us. Once we really take that to heart—and remember what our job is—we'll find it hard to point a finger at others.

My friend, God judges all of us according to our hearts—and only God can see our hearts. We don't need to examine everyone's motives and worry about whether they have it right. Honestly, I don't have the time or the energy or the ability to do that. I'd rather spend my days playing golf with my husband or singing in the car with my kids. And it really isn't any of our business. God is big enough to take care of what is wrong with the world.

So is it ever okay to point out sin or pay attention to wrong-doing in a fellow believer? Yes. The Bible even spells out how we are to respond to different kinds of offenses. Matthew 18:15-17, for instance, outlines a way to deal with a Christian brother who has wronged us:

> If another believer sins against you, go privately and point out the offense. If the other person listens and confesses it, you have won that person back. But if you are unsuccessful, take one or two others with you and go back again, so that everything you say may be confirmed by two or three witnesses. If the person still

refuses to listen, take your case to the church. Then if
he or she won't accept the church's decision, treat that
person as a pagan or a corrupt tax collector (NLT).

Other passages such as 1 Corinthians 5:1-5, Galatians 6:1-3,
and Titus 3:9-11 tackle the issue of egregious, ongoing, disrup-
tive sin within a church community. And there are numerous
examples of God speaking through a prophet to point out sin
in his people.

But none of these passages, in my opinion, bears any resem-
blance to the petty, graceless sniping and judgmental attitude
of a critical heart. The emphasis is always on grace, forbear-
ance, forgiveness, and eventual restoration. At the very worst,
believers are counseled to disassociate with an egregious and
unrepentant sinner with the purpose of eventually seeing him
or her restored to fellowship.

There is a big difference, in other words, between loving a
brother back to life and beating the life out of him. There is a
big difference between pointing out ongoing sin in the life of
a sister for the purpose of bringing her back into fellowship
and shooting arrow after arrow of criticism for the purpose of
punishing someone who hasn't lived up to my standards. And
there is a really big difference between sharing a word from God
and hitting others over the head with a prejudice or a personal
opinion.

In all our dealings with others, a gracious spirit can go a
long way. The wisdom of Proverbs is a good reminder: "Pleasant
words are as a honeycomb, sweet to the mind and healing to the
body" (16:24, AMP). And "a soft answer turns away wrath, but
grievous words stir up anger" (15:1, AMP).

The Antidote to a Critical Spirit

Philip Yancey, who is one of my favorite authors, once wrote something intriguing about his own legalistic experience growing up and what he learned from G. K. Chesterton.

> I had conceived of faith as a tight-lipped, grim exercise of spiritual discipline, a blending of asceticism and rationalism in which joy leaked away. Chesterton restored to me a thirst for the exuberance that flows from a link to the God who dreamed up all the things that give me pleasure.[4]

What a wonderful thought—and what a powerful antidote to the critical spirit. Some of us would never dare to think that God has actually dreamed up things for our pleasure. But I do. In fact, the other day, this idea nearly overwhelmed me with joy. Philly and I were at the movies, and right before the feature started, a commercial came on. The screen filled up as if it were a big glass, ice cubes started dropping in, and Coca-Cola came raining down.

Philly looked at me and grinned. "That makes you happy, doesn't it, babe?"

I just grinned back and nodded.

Then a thought hit me. I pulled Philly toward me and murmured in his ear, "What if when we get to heaven, we walk into our mansions and everything we've ever loved is waiting right there for us? Even things we've forgotten."

I thought of my Maggie dog, my little Miss Independent. I thought of my granny standing there with her apron on, fried chicken sizzling in a cast-iron skillet on the stove, and an ice-cold bottle of Coke held out in her hand, just for me. My mind raced, envisioning my Father creating all that for my pleasure.

But so many of us don't know God that way. We just think of God as one who whacks us if we don't get it right, belittles us if we make a mistake, or criticizes us if we do something other than go to church, read our Bibles, or serve on committees.

I am so grateful I've gotten to know God a little better in the past few years. His net is wide. And his strength is perfect in my weakness. I have known his grace, and I passionately want to give my heart to him.

What if the next time you encounter something or someone who annoys or irritates you, instead of criticizing, you try offering a gentle word that is as sweet as honeycomb? The next time you get a waitress who doesn't give you much more than a grunt, try speaking a word of kindness. Let her know you're not in a hurry, that you just want her to take her time.

Try it. See what that does to her attitude.

It's so easy to be a critic, to speak harshly out of our own pain and selfishness.

But to love people, to believe the best of them, to open ourselves to the abundant grace God lavishes on each one of us every day, and to extend grace just as lavishly to others—that takes an open, alive heart.

And that, my friend, is the heart God is after.

CHAPTER EIGHT

THE SHAMED HEART

Maybe it wasn't relief she was feeling, but shame.
Both made you burn from the inside out.
JODI PICOULT

SHE CAME UP TO ME at the end of Bible study one week. I can still see her face. She didn't smile. Rarely was she able to look me in my eyes when she spoke to me. I got to know her better over breakfast the next day. I listened to her story of abuse. Even after we said good-bye, I couldn't get her out of my mind.

Gifted? Oh, amazingly.

Potential? Out the wazoo.

Full of shame? Heartbreakingly so.

In fact, her story confirmed to me that I was to teach next on that subject.

The Box of Shame

One of our favorite movies to watch as a family on road trips is *Despicable Me*. Our girls love the orphans in the story, and our boy, not surprisingly, is captivated by the little yellow minions with the ridiculous laughs and extreme bodily function noises. Philly and I just think it's a funny story. But one scene always sticks in my mind. It's the one where the girls arrive back at the orphanage after an expedition to sell their version of Girl Scout cookies. They haven't done well, and the horrible orphanage lady (think Miss Hannigan from *Annie*) scolds them. Then she tells them they'd better improve next time if they don't want to be put in the "box of shame."

As they leave, they have to pass a cardboard box sitting by the door of the office. From inside, a little girl says hi through a cutout hole in the box. And sure enough, written in marker across the front are the words *Box of Shame*.

Have you ever done time in the box of shame, trapped by the painful sense that there is something badly wrong with you? I certainly have, and I know plenty of men and women and even children who have been there too. Some have spent their whole lives that way.

Yet interestingly enough, the first mention of shame in the Bible is not about its ubiquitous presence but about its gaping absence. "Adam and his wife were both naked, and they felt *no shame*" (Genesis 2:25, NIV, emphasis added).

Think of that. There was a season in the history of this planet when shame was completely unknown. Never felt. Never experienced. Then Satan showed up with his lie. Adam and Eve believed it. And shame entered the human experience.

> At that moment their eyes were opened, and they
> suddenly felt shame at their nakedness. So they sewed
> fig leaves together to cover themselves.
> When the cool evening breezes were blowing, the
> man and his wife heard the LORD God walking about

in the garden. So they hid from the LORD God among the trees.

GENESIS 3:7-8, NLT

Why were they hiding? Because they were ashamed.

Shut Down by Shame

The first man and woman came into this world fully alive, totally connected to their hearts and to their God. But when they left the Garden, they were weighed down with shame. Sadly, that journey from innocence to shame is a familiar one for many of us. How does it happen? How do we go from that child's heart we came into the world with to a heart shut down by shame?

For many of us, shame is our default mode, if you will. It feels like a built-in part of us. And it usually comes from something that has been done to us—maybe verbal, physical, or sexual abuse. The imprints of those wounds convince us that in some way we were responsible for the midnight stalker or the afternoon tyrant. And in our inability to discern truth from lie, our hearts are racked with shame. Even if we know better, our hearts are convinced that we somehow deserved it—because we were weak and didn't make them stop or because there was something wrong with us that invited the abuse. We might have even been told by the abuser or by those we turned to for help that the whole thing was really our fault. And the heart of shame was established.

Others of us grew up feeling shame over the fact that we existed at all. We internalized the message that we were in the way or that other people's problems existed because of us. Or maybe, like the three orphans in *Despicable Me*, we felt shame over the fact that we weren't valuable enough to be loved, kept, or treasured. We developed a shamed heart because we allowed the enemy to convince us that we were an inconvenience, a mistake, a drain.

Still others of us grew up being shamed for the things we did, even when those things were just accidents or when we were too young or inexperienced to do better. Statements like "You're so stupid," "You're an idiot," "You never do anything right," or "You'll never amount to anything" woke us up in the morning and tucked us in at night.

And for many of us, our guilt and regret over past decisions or actions have contributed to a shamed heart. Or rather, the way we responded to our guilt and regret has kept us trapped in shame.

It is important to know that guilt and regret are meant to go hand in hand with a wonderful tool called conviction. Conviction is our friend. It is Jesus' gracious tool to move us away from things we shouldn't do. I call it "the tug." It is that pull I feel on my heart when the Holy Spirit is letting me know something isn't right. Sometimes I'll feel the tug when I'm about to do something I shouldn't—say an unkind word, do a wrongful action, or even think an unclean thought. The Spirit tugs at me to change direction. Or maybe conviction will weigh in over somewhere I've already allowed my heart to go: those critical thoughts, those controlling actions, those performing moments. And so he tugs me with his conviction, allowing me to experience guilt or regret over my choice and then to repent.

The apostle Paul refers to guilt combined with conviction as "godly grief":

> For godly grief and the pain God is permitted to direct, produce a repentance that leads and contributes to salvation and deliverance from evil, and it never brings regret; but worldly grief (the hopeless sorrow that is

DENISE HILDRETH JONES

characteristic of the pagan world) is deadly [breeding
and ending in death].

2 CORINTHIANS 7:10, AMP

See, godly grief is created to bring us to repentance, and
it never brings shame. But if we *stay* in the place of "worldly
grief"—experiencing guilt or regret without being freed through
repentance and God's forgiveness—that is when the enemy can
get a foothold and move us into a place of shame.

Trust me, if you are experiencing shame, that's a telltale sign
the enemy has found himself a clear passageway to your heart.
God uses conviction. He has not and does not use shame.

But maybe that is where life has landed you. Maybe the guilt
and regret over something you've done or said—or wished you'd
done or said—has left you languishing in the box of shame.
Maybe it was an affair or an abortion, an addiction or a bankruptcy. Maybe it was a word spoken in haste or a word not
spoken at all. And for whatever reason, the experience has left
you with that sense of being deeply damaged and unworthy. So
you too have landed in the box of shame.

It wouldn't even surprise me if, as you read this book and
identify certain unhealthy choices, Satan tries to entangle you
with shame. He is so good at twisting even our best intentions—
and God's sweet, convicting presence—into something that is
shameful.

Why? Because he knows shame can paralyze us. Cripple us.
Render us of no effect. And isn't that his greatest desire?

Which is why a shamed heart, like all the others, is a sin.

How We Hide

Shame's goal? To make us hide, just as Adam and Eve did in the
Garden. They hid their naked bodies behind fig leaves. Then,

when they heard God coming, they jumped into the bushes to hide from their Creator's presence.

We humans have been hiding ever since. In fact, some of us do it literally.

I'm thinking of a certain young woman I have known for years. Over time, I noticed a pattern of behavior with her—and remember, patterns are very telling. When this woman is really ready to have a friend who will be honest with her, she'll seek me out. But when she is doing things and living in a way she doesn't want me to know about, she goes AWOL—I mean, completely off the map. And that is what some people do with a shamed heart. They literally hide. They dissociate from anyone who will speak real truth. As Beth Moore wrote in her book *When Godly People Do Ungodly Things*, "Satan loves isolation. He wants to draw the believer out of healthy relationships into isolated relationships and out of healthy practices into secretive, unhealthy practices."[1]

Physically disappearing isn't the only way to hide, of course. Some attempt it by changing their bodies. For instance, hiding may well be an unconscious motivation behind eating disorders. Those suffering from anorexia nervosa may "eat less and less in an effort to become smaller and smaller because of their self-effacing desire to simply disappear."[2]

On the other end of the spectrum, many who have been sexually abused or bullied will tell you they began overeating in a desire to hide.

> Those who suffered sexual abuse at a young age often develop deep-rooted fears and insecurities in their subconscious, which in turn manifest as a desire to become and/or stay obese in a subconscious attempt to be less attractive or desirable and thereby fend off any

future abuse. In this sense, obesity can make a person feel safer and more secure since [it shields] them from unwanted attention.[3]

Addictions, too, can have a hiding component. Whether the addiction is to drugs, alcohol, sex, shopping, plastic surgery, or eating, rather than confronting life and relationships directly, addicts typically retreat into their dependencies, relying on substances or experiences to numb their pain or distract them with pleasure. In the process, unfortunately, they play into the lies of the enemy: "This is what you really are" or "This is all you're really worth."

Some hide in other people. They gravitate toward people who seem stronger than they are and may seek their value in being close to these kinds of personalities. Their sense of self-worth then relies on a codependent relationship they have allowed to swallow them whole. Why? Because shame keeps them from thinking they have anything to offer a relationship. These people are special prey to those with controlling hearts, who love to use shame or guilt as manipulation tools.

Still others hide in many of the ways we've talked about already. We may hide by performing, by trying to control our environment, by criticizing and attacking others or ourselves—all in an effort to somehow escape that underlying sense of shame. I've said it multiple times: all of these hearts can intersect with one another on any given day and at any given time.

Perhaps the most common form of hiding involves keeping secrets—concealing the parts of us we believe to be shameful beneath the surface of our lives. It could be something relatively small—a dirty house or an unpaid bill. Or it could be something major—a bankruptcy, a hoarding problem, addiction, abuse, mental illness. It could be an individual secret we keep from everyone or a family secret we've been taught to hold close from childhood. ("Don't tell anyone about . . .") But whatever it is, we expend a lot of energy making sure it stays hidden so that no one knows the painful truth about who we think we are. In hiding our secrets, we also seek to hide from our shame.

The Lie of the Shamed Heart: "God Can't Love or Use Me Because I'm No Good"

The lie of the shamed heart strikes at the very core of who we believe we are, trying to convince us that God can't love or use us because we're just no good. Now this may sound similar to the performing heart and the critical heart. And indeed there are similarities, but there are also important distinctions.

The lie of the performing heart is *I'm not enough the way God made me . . . so I have to fake it*. A discomfort with our authentic heart leads us to act *as if* we were someone else.

The lie of the critical heart is *God wants me to get it right*. Our misconception about God's expectations results in an exaggerated focus on who is right and who is wrong.

But the shamed heart is haunted by an even more basic sense of being damaged or inferior goods—unworthy, valueless, unsuitable, even soiled. And doesn't the enemy love to accuse us of being just that? He knows that the more we believe it, the less impact we can make for the Kingdom of God.

So what have we forgotten in this lie? We have forgotten that we are made in God's image.

> Then God said, "Let us make mankind in our image,
> in our likeness, so that they may rule over the fish in
> the sea and the birds in the sky, over the livestock and
> all the wild animals, and over all the creatures that
> move along the ground."

So God created mankind in his own image,
in the image of God he created them;
male and female he created them.

GENESIS 1:26-27, NIV

Does it get any higher quality than that? How can we not
have value when we were created in the image of the Creator
himself? And yet the enemy of our hearts would try to convince
us that we were created in the image of something broken or
damaged. Oh, what a liar he is! And how deadly the fallout of
the shamed heart can be—because that basic lie can spawn one
false belief after another that not only keeps us trapped in the
box of shame but can also endanger our very souls.

The first of these false conclusions is that we have to be good
enough before we can encounter Christ. But the truth is that
none of us will ever be good enough. You might want to read
that one more time: we will *never* be good enough. So we have
to come to him just as we are. With all our messed-upness!

Christ . . . presented himself for this sacrificial death
when we were far too weak and rebellious to do anything
to get ourselves ready. And even if we hadn't been so
weak, we wouldn't have known what to do anyway. We
can understand someone dying for a person worth dying
for, and we can understand how someone good and
noble could inspire us to selfless sacrifice. But God put
his love on the line for us by offering his Son in sacrificial
death while we were of no use whatever to him.

ROMANS 5:6-8, *The Message*

It doesn't get any clearer than that! If Jesus' blood doesn't
cover our sin, then his death is a farce.

The enemy also tries to convince us that because we are not good enough, we should hide and not have communion with God. Have you ever noticed that when your heart is encased in shame, the last place you want to be is in the presence of God? Isn't it ironic that the enemy of our hearts can layer us in shame and keep us out of the presence of the One who takes away all shame?

And here's an especially subtle and dangerous false belief. The enemy also tries to convince our shamed hearts that the blood Jesus spilled for us on the cross wasn't good enough. That's not just a lie; it's an insult to God! The apostle Paul blows it out of the water:

> Adam, who got us into this, also points ahead to the One who will get us out of it.
>
> Yet the rescuing gift is not exactly parallel to the death-dealing sin. If one man's sin put crowds of people at the dead-end abyss of separation from God, just think what God's gift poured through one man, Jesus Christ, will do! There's no comparison between that death-dealing sin and this generous, life-giving gift. The verdict on that one sin was the death sentence; the verdict on the many sins that followed was this wonderful life sentence. If death got the upper hand through one man's wrongdoing, can you imagine the breathtaking recovery life makes, sovereign life, in those who grasp with both hands this wildly extravagant life-gift, this grand setting-everything-right, that the one man Jesus Christ provides?
>
> Here it is in a nutshell: Just as one person did it wrong and got us in all this trouble with sin and death, another person did it right and got us out of it. But

more than just getting us out of trouble, he got us into life!

ROMANS 5:14-18, *The Message*

Reclaiming the Shamed Heart

Do you remember the first question God asked Adam and Eve after they ate the fruit from the tree? He asked them, "Where are you?"

He knew where Adam and Eve were. But he needed *them* to know where they were. He needed them to recognize their sin, their separation.

And that is what he needs some of us to do today. Where are you? Do you know? Are you willing to admit it? It is the first step in reclaiming the shamed heart. And without it there is no moving forward.

The next step? We need to get honest, stop hiding, and step out of the bushes. Which means we need to open up and admit our secrets and our sins.

Recently a friend shared with me a visual aid that a counselor uses in sessions with people who are dealing with activities or issues that lead to shame. The counselor drew a big circle, like a clock face, and wrote the word *shame* at the top, in the twelve o'clock position. At about the four o'clock position, she wrote the word *thought*, and she wrote *action* at eight o'clock. Then she traced a big black line around the circle to show how we go from shamed feelings to shamed thoughts to actions that both reflect our shame and result in *more* feelings of shame, more thoughts of shame, and so on, in a truly vicious circle.

The counselor continued to draw around and around until she had created a thick black circle. She asked, "What happens when you create a cycle of behavior like this?"

The answer was "isolation"—which is always the enemy's goal. He wants us hiding from God and others.

Then the counselor drew a line to break through the consuming circle and said, "The one thing that breaks up this cycle of shame, thought, and then action is . . ."

Are you ready for the word? It isn't superspiritual. It wasn't *pray* or *fast* or *read* (your Bible). The word was deceptively simple: *talk*. Just *talk*.

Have you ever noticed how as soon as you tell a friend, a real friend, something you've been going through, you feel as if the weight of the world has fallen off your shoulders? One of my huge personal places of accountability is that if there is ever anything I don't want to share with my closest friends, then I know it is something I *need* to share. If not, the enemy will wreak havoc with me.

My friend Deneen and I have done this for years, telling each other those deepest secrets so the enemy can't use them against us. I know that every time I dare to talk about my secrets, something amazing happens. I can actually feel my perspective shift, feel myself break free of what the enemy has been doing to me.

The reason the enemy loves to keep us in hiding, living with our secrets, is that then his is the only voice we hear. And we all know where that will ultimately lead.

King David knew firsthand the danger of keeping secrets. After his affair with Bathsheba and the murder of her husband, Uriah, he wrote these words: "When I kept silent, my bones grew old through my groaning all the day long. For day and night Your hand was heavy upon me; my vitality was turned into the drought of summer" (Psalm 32:3-4).

Look at the terms he used: *groaning, all the day long, heavy, drought.* This is what secrets produce. This is their legacy. And this is where you may be if there are hidden places of shame in your heart. You may never have entered what my friend Ken Edwards describes as "the reality of your own life."

I'm sure you have your reasons. Maybe you like your secret. Maybe you're simply not ready to get rid of this piece of your life that you're hiding. Or you may be afraid—afraid of the pain, afraid of what life would look like without this secret, afraid of failure if you even try to break free. But until you are willing to confront what you are hiding from, you will never reclaim your heart.

It's time. It's time to get honest and dare to bring your secrets into the light. There is such power in simply admitting the broken places of our lives. In fact, I have learned that until we are willing to admit where we are, we are preventing God from helping us.

That doesn't mean we admit our secrets to everybody. Revealing our secrets and admitting our sin aren't the same as blogging our most painful failures for everyone to see or standing in front of the church and letting it all hang out. A counselor, a pastor, or a very close friend can be a safe choice—but even the counselor, pastor, or friend needs to be chosen carefully. Author Tammy Maltby suggests some helpful guidelines for discernment in her book *The God Who Sees You*:

- *What is prudent?* It really isn't safe or wise to share certain realities in certain areas—or with certain people.
- *What is the right time to reveal secrets?* Sometimes patience is a wiser strategy.
- *What might the consequences be?* Have I counted the cost of revealing a secret?
- *Whom should I tell?* Who can be trusted? Who needs to be protected?

- ◆ *Whose secret is it?* Each person is responsible for his or her own heart and relationship with God.
- ◆ *What are my motives?* Is there a hint of vengeance, bitterness, or glee in my truth telling? Do I hope to get an edge in some dispute?
- ◆ *What is God saying to me?* Prayerful listening always helps.
- ◆ *Most of all . . . what would love do?* Because isn't love God's ultimate criteria?[4]

However we choose to reveal our shame to other people, we definitely need to get honest before the Lord. Unless we go to him with our secrets and our sins, lay them before him, and ask for his forgiveness, we will never find freedom from the box of shame.

That's exactly what David did when the prophet Nathan confronted him about his adultery with Bathsheba and the murder of her husband. David immediately admitted to Nathan, "I have sinned against the LORD" (2 Samuel 12:13). And then he poured his heart out before God:

> Have mercy upon me, O God,
> According to Your lovingkindness;
> According to the multitude of Your tender mercies,
> Blot out my transgressions.
> Wash me thoroughly from my iniquity,
> And cleanse me from my sin.
>
> For I acknowledge my transgressions,
> And my sin is always before me.
> Against You, You only, have I sinned,
> And done this evil in Your sight.
> PSALM 51:1-4

David's sin—adultery and murder—was pretty obvious. He obviously needed to repent and be forgiven. But shame doesn't always result from personal transgression. What do we do with shame over a sin someone else committed against us? We can be honest about it and tell the secret.

For instance, being a victim of abuse isn't sin. It is heartbreaking, and it has broken the heart of your Father, but it's not sin. But choosing to stay in a box of shame over the abuse is a sin. Trusting Satan's lies over God's Word of Truth is a sin. And shame over something that's been done to you can shut down your heart just as effectively as shame over something you have done.

I know people still living in their little boxes of shame twenty years after an event that caused them the shame in the first place. And that is sin because it is something we have chosen to continue. We could have lifted the top off that box years ago and climbed out. The person who put us there left the room years ago.

Work to Do

One of the most powerful stories in the Bible is the story of Simon Peter's denial of Jesus. I can't imagine that anyone in all of Scripture felt more shame than Peter did at that moment.

After all, he had an especially intimate relationship with Jesus. One of the very first disciples chosen, he'd been at his Lord's side for the important moments of Jesus' ministry. Jesus had even taken him into some of the secret places where not all the disciples got to go. He was on the Mount of Transfiguration. He was in the garden of Gethsemane. Jesus had even visited his home.

But then came that traumatic moment when a frightened, confused Peter denied that he even knew Jesus. He did it three times, just as Jesus had said he would. According to Luke's account, Jesus turned and looked at Peter after the third denial, and Peter suddenly remembered Jesus' prediction.

Can you even imagine the shame of betraying someone you knew so intimately and loved so deeply—someone your heart desired to please, to serve, to honor? To do it not just once, but three times, and then to look the other person in the eye after you've done it?

That moment couldn't help but have a huge impact on Peter's heart. In fact, have you ever noticed that not one Gospel account depicts Peter as being on the scene when Jesus was crucified? I guess it's possible that the Gospels just don't happen to mention his presence. But I really believe he was AWOL. Gone. Vamoosed. He just couldn't handle the shame.

And what happened then? If I were writing this story from my fiction writer's perspective and my oh-so-human heart, I would have finished Peter's story very differently. I would have had Jesus giving up on Peter, sending him a "You're fired"—if he sent him anything at all. I might have even added some scenes after Jesus rose from the dead when he went out and told everyone what Peter had done and what a disappointment he was. What a pitiful excuse for a friend. What a lost cause. That's how my humanness would write the aftermath of such betrayal. In fact, I've probably spun out my own stories of betrayal much the same way. Haven't you?

But this is one time, yet again, that I'm grateful Jesus doesn't do things at all the way we would. In Mark's account, after Jesus' resurrection, an angel greets Mary and the other women at the tomb. Do you know what he tells her?

"Don't be alarmed," he said. "You are looking for Jesus the Nazarene, who was crucified. He has risen! He is not here. See the place where they laid him. But go, tell his disciples and Peter, 'He is going ahead of you into Galilee. There you will see him, just as he told you.'"

MARK 16:6-7, NIV

Peter is singled out for receiving the most wonderful, most astounding news anyone will ever get. No other disciples are mentioned by name. How telling is that of Jesus' great compassion and love toward us?

John's account tells us what happened the next time Peter met Jesus (John 21). It happened when Peter was out fishing. Why was he fishing? I can think of several possible reasons.

Remember, Peter was fishing the first time Jesus found him. So I can't help but wonder, considering Peter's deep love for Jesus, whether part of him thought Jesus might find him there again. Which might be a message to many of us who struggle with shame. Maybe we need to go back to where we met Jesus the first time.

But I believe there was also an element of hiding out in this moment for Peter. Peter had been Jesus' disciple for three years. He had been called to do something powerful for the Kingdom of God. And yet, in his shame, he might have chosen to hide in what was familiar. Fishing might have been his version of putting on a fig leaf and jumping into the bushes.

But look how persistent God is. Peter hid in his fishing boat (taking some other disciples with him), but Jesus showed up right on shore. He called out to Peter and the others in the boat, "Friends, haven't you any fish?" (v. 5, NIV).

They didn't. Not a one. They didn't even know whom they were talking to.

So Jesus told them what he'd told them in the past—to throw their net on the other side of the boat. And when they did, they couldn't contain the haul. The net was absolutely bulging with fish—so full they couldn't pull it into the boat.

John got it immediately: "It is the Lord!" (v. 7).

And do you know what Peter did? He did what any shamed heart desperately longing for Jesus' forgiveness and freedom does. He jumped out of the boat and started swimming for shore as fast as he could. When he got there, he discovered that Jesus hadn't written him off at all. Nope. In fact, he'd made breakfast for Peter and the other disciples.

But Jesus didn't stop there—and this is crucial to realize. He went on to redeem Peter's shame by reminding him of his purpose.

Three times he asked Peter if he loved him. Three times Peter assured him that he did. And three times Jesus told Peter, "Feed my sheep."

How many times had Peter denied Jesus? That's right. Say it out loud: *three*.

For each denial Peter had made, Jesus gave him the chance to redeem his shame, then reminded him that he had work to do.

And Peter believed him, big-time. He believed so completely that, after the Day of Pentecost, he preached the world's first revival, inspiring three thousand people to give their hearts to Jesus.

How Do You See Me?

What if Peter had chosen to live in his shame instead of responding to Jesus? What if he had jumped out of that boat and swum in the opposite direction? If he had refused to believe that Jesus still had something for him to do? If, instead of being present on the Day of Pentecost, he'd just surrendered himself to a life of fishing, convincing himself that was all he was worth? What would have been lost? And what might be lost for you and me while we are hiding in our shame?

I'm pretty clear on what would have been lost for me. This book you're holding in your hands, for starters. You see, after my divorce, I was all but overcome with shame. I wore it like a cloak. I felt that instead of a scarlet *A* on my chest, I wore a scarlet *D*, and it wasn't for Denise. I really believed that my divorce was all people saw when they looked at me.

Remember, I came from a denomination that debated whether divorced people could be on the deacon board, let alone be ministers of the gospel of Jesus Christ. I had judged divorced people all my life. I had fought against divorce with everything I had, but I had failed. Talk about feeling like damaged goods! What could life possibly hold for me now?

How ironic is that? I went from assuming I only needed half a cross (before my divorce) to feeling that even a full cross wasn't enough to take away my shame. Only the enemy of my heart could do that.

So one day, in Ken Edwards's office, I started reciting my litany of shame—how bad I felt about my divorce, how I thought God couldn't use me and so on and so on. Ken had heard it all before, many times, and he'd always listened patiently. But that day he did something he had never done before. He sat on the edge of his chair with fire in his eyes—a kind of righteous anger. He leaned in and said, "Denise, you've got to get over this."

That got my attention. I kind of sat there with my mouth open while Ken went on. "I don't see you as a divorced woman," he said. "I see you as a beautiful woman who has such a heart for God. And God does not see you as a divorced woman either. He is hurt that it happened, but he doesn't see that when he looks at you. He sees you as his beloved, someone he died to save, someone he's forgiven, someone whose life he wants to use for his glory. And it's about time you start taking that seriously. So the next time all these thoughts want to come up, I want you to ask yourself, 'Where is God with me in this moment? And how does he feel about me?'"

I had learned by then that when Ken spoke, I needed to listen. So I did what he suggested. I began to ask God again and again—especially when those feelings of shame washed over me—"How do you see me? How do you feel about me?"

I was amazed at his response. Through all sorts of circumstances, he reassured my heart that I was valued and loved . . . and that he still had a plan for me. But the choice of whether I would follow that plan or continue to live in shame was mine.

And it is yours as well. Whether you choose to spend the rest of your life hiding in your box of shame is your decision. It isn't a decision you can blame anyone else for. Why would you want to when God has so much out there just waiting for you?

Look at the way the prophet Isaiah describes God's plans for his people:

> But you shall be called the priests of the Lord; people will speak of you as the ministers of our God. You shall eat the wealth of the nations, and the glory [once that of your captors] shall be yours.
>
> *Instead of your [former] shame you shall have a twofold recompense; instead of dishonor and reproach [your people] shall rejoice in their portion.* Therefore in their land they shall possess double [what they had forfeited]; everlasting joy shall be theirs.
>
> For I the Lord love justice; I hate robbery and wrong with violence or a burnt offering. And I will

faithfully give them their recompense in truth, and I
will make an everlasting covenant or league with them.

And their offspring shall be known among the
nations and their descendants among the peoples. All
who see them [in their prosperity] will recognize and
acknowledge that they are the people whom the Lord
has blessed.

ISAIAH 61:6-9, AMP (EMPHASIS ADDED)

Did you see that? For your *former* shame, you will receive
double.

Yes, once we allow our shame to move from our present to
our past, where it belongs, we will receive a double blessing.
And instead of the "dishonor and reproach" we have lived in,
we shall rejoice over what God has given us.

In the next chapter, Isaiah goes on:

You shall also be [so beautiful and prosperous as to be
thought of as] a crown of glory and honor in the hand
of the Lord, and a royal diadem [exceedingly beautiful]
in the hand of your God.

You [Judah] shall no more be termed Forsaken,
nor shall your land be called Desolate any more. But
you shall be called Hephzibah [My delight is in her],
and your land be called Beulah [married]; for the Lord
delights in you, and your land shall be married [owned
and protected by the Lord].

For as a young man marries a virgin [O Jerusalem],
so shall your sons marry you; and as the bridegroom
rejoices over the bride, so shall your God rejoice
over you.

ISAIAH 62:3-5, AMP

We haven't thought we were worth anything. And here we are told that we're going to be "a crown of glory and honor in the hand of the Lord." If God thinks that of us, how can we think anything less?

Can I share something with you? There may always be people who don't think you are worth much. They may see only your failures, only your sins, only the wrong things you have done. They may even determine that you have nothing of value to offer them. But that is about their hearts, not yours. It doesn't have anything to do with what God sees when he looks at you.

This is the God who thought you up in the first place. This is the God who redeemed you, who forgives your sins, who wants you involved in his plans for the world. He delights in you. He rejoices over you. He values you

- in spite of one marriage or two marriages or three marriages;
- in spite of the abortion or the adultery or the betrayal in your past;
- in spite of the sexual abuse or parental neglect;
- in spite of financial failure and irresponsibility;
- in spite of what you've done . . . and what has been done to you;
- even in spite of the shame you've wallowed in for so long.

How long has it been since you believed that? Maybe it's time you stopped hiding and believed it again. Because he has not called us to live in boxes of shame. He has called us to live in wide-open spaces where he delights in us. He has called us to walk in the forgiveness and freedom that his death so beautifully bought. He has called us to walk in his way and follow him.

Will we ever be good enough? *No!*

But was Jesus' sacrifice good enough? *Absolutely!*

This issue needs to be settled. If your shame keeps lingering, I'll tell you what Ken told me: you've just got to get over it.

Because "if the Son sets you free, you are free through and through" (John 8:36, *The Message*).

CHAPTER NINE

THE ANGRY HEART

Get mad, then get over it.
COLIN POWELL

I DIDN'T WANT to teach this lesson. It wasn't on my list. And let me tell you, I like lists. I like plans. I like a lot of things the Lord hasn't allowed me to hold on to during this season.

Then I got an e-mail from a friend who asked me, "Have you talked about the angry heart yet? Because that's where I am."

"Nuh-uh," I said. "Not doing that one. I want to do the people-pleasing heart and the rescuing heart and the distracted heart. If I keep on adding hearts, this book is going to end up as the *Encyclopedia Britannica* of hearts. Anyway, the shamed heart already messed me up, and I don't have time for any more kinks in my wheel."

By the title of the chapter, you can see how well that worked out for me.

But what I realized is this lesson might not have been written for anyone else but me.

The awareness surfaced after I taught on the shamed heart. The entire previous week, while I was preparing the shamed heart lesson, I kept encountering folks who told me how angry they were. Then on the night after the lesson, my husband walked into the closet, where I was getting ready for bed. He proceeded to share with me some of his struggles over the past month with frustration, fear, avoidance . . . and anger. Then he put words to it: "Babe, I think I'm one of those angry hearts you've been talking about."

So the next morning, still clothed in my pj's, I sat down and wrote out my lesson. It came easily. Too easily.

Could it be that it takes an angry heart to know one?

Angry Expressions

Rage is probably the most obvious expression of anger. Angry people turn red in the face. They lay on the horn or flip you off. They pull hair. They shake their fists—or use them. They may break objects, slam doors, beat people up. This kind of anger is never pretty. In fact, it can look like what Jesus saw in the demon-possessed man who lived in the caves. It can be crazy and out of control.

Other angry people use words as weapons. Their speech is stinging and mean, degrading and abusive, snide and sarcastic, or downright cruel. And make no mistake. Angry words can be as damaging as a fist or a knife.

Seeking revenge is a common response to anger. The specific action may vary from an embarrassing text message to physical violence. But the angry impulse behind the action is the same: "You hurt me, I'll hurt you back." Revenge is punitive by nature.

It's probably helpful to note that any of these expressions of anger can be displaced. Instead of responding to whatever provoked the anger in the first place, the angry person takes it out on whatever or whoever happens to be in the way. The recipient of the resulting outburst may be completely innocent or guilty of a very small offense—nothing to justify the flood of fury that comes down on his or her head.

I have a friend, for instance, whose life has been difficult and painful. She lost her mother at a young age, is alienated from her family, suffers severe health problems, and barely ekes out a living on Social Security. She lives with a lot of pent-up anger, and most of the time she handles it well. But occasionally she has a bad customer service experience, and then it all comes out. Many a poor phone operator has had to endure her mostly displaced wrath.

Some people express their anger through an excessive need to control. I remember sitting in Ken's office one day, distraught over a person in my life who was going to great lengths to marginalize me. This person had been hurt (not by me!) and the resulting anger showed itself in extremely controlling behavior. Unfortunately this controller did have some say over what happened in my life; I had little choice about that. All I could do was try to handle my own anger in a healthy way.

My typical response to anger is to withdraw. This was a pattern in my first marriage and one that could easily have carried over into my second marriage. However, as I mentioned in an earlier chapter, I quickly realized that I could not go back to the old patterns. I had to learn to express my anger and not let it shut down my heart.

Withdrawing is a kind of inward-directed anger, but there are others. Some angry people hide from their anger in unhealthy or excessive behavior. Inappropriate sex, indulgence in porn, overeating or drinking too much, vegging out in front of the television—any vice you can think of can be a way of responding to anger.

For others, anger reveals itself through health issues. Quite a few studies have been done on the damage that unresolved anger and unforgiveness (a form of unresolved anger) can do to a body. Anger can precipitate any number of physical and mental illnesses, including cancer, heart disease, and clinical depression. Many counselors now are looking at the spiritual roots of diseases, believing there is often a heart issue connected to the physical issues we face—and the heart involved is often an angry, bitter, unforgiving one.[1]

Is Anger a Sin?

Anger is not always a negative or destructive force, however. At its most basic, anger is just an emotion generated automatically by the body in response to a perceived threat. It's part of our built-in fight-or-flight response to danger. Our bodies release hormones to energize us to respond to the threat, and the emotion of anger is part of the "fight" response. (Fear accompanies the "flight" response.)

Feeling anger, in other words, is simply part of being human. It's a natural reaction when we are hurt or threatened. But there's another element in anger that I believe is part of the image of God in us—a built-in response to evil and injustice. According to Psalm 7, "God is angry with the wicked every day" (v. 11). And because we are created in God's image, there is a part of us that is innately designed to respond the same way.

The energy that accompanies anger, in other words, can actually be a positive force. There really is such a thing as righteous anger that spurs us to fight what is wrong. Jesus himself responded to the money changers in the Temple with this kind of anger. I believe he wants us to respond with anger when we see people being hurt and exploited. And as I'll make clear later in this chapter, I believe we're *supposed* to be angry at the one who caused all this trouble in the first place—the enemy of our souls.

Anger, in other words, is not a sin in itself.

Even responding in anger is not *always* a sin.

But an angry heart—one that loses control on a regular basis or allows bitterness and resentment and festering fury to shut it down—that is most definitely a sin.

Why Are We So Angry?

If anger is a built-in response to a perceived threat, it follows that a variety of circumstances—and perceptions—can make us angry. For instance, anger sometimes stems from disappointment. That happened to Job at one point. And why wouldn't he be angry? He'd lost everything—his possessions, his family, even his health—and then his "friends" arrived to pontificate and pass judgment. I bet he wished he had an "unfriend" button. *He* didn't even understand why he was where he was. He told his friends, "Put up with me while I speak. After I've spoken, you can make fun of me! . . . Why shouldn't I be angry and uneasy?" (Job 21:3-4, NIrV).

Disappointment can make you angry.

Others come to have angry hearts through their own sin.

One of the best biblical examples of sin and anger is King Saul. Saul wasted his opportunity as king because of his obsession with control and recognition as well as his unwillingness to obey God. And it all began the day a young kid named David showed up and killed a giant named Goliath, who was terrorizing and taunting God's people. The entire nation had an intense response to David's accomplishment. But Saul's reaction was even more intense:

As they returned home, after David had killed the Philistine, the women poured out of all the villages of Israel singing and dancing, welcoming King Saul with tambourines, festive songs, and lutes. In playful frolic the women sang,

Saul kills by the thousand,
David by the ten thousand!

This made Saul angry—very angry. He took it as a personal insult. He said, "They credit David with 'ten thousands' and me with only 'thousands.' Before you know it they'll be giving him the kingdom!" From that moment on, Saul kept his eye on David.

1 SAMUEL 18:6-9, *The Message*

Saul's sin of envy led him to develop an angry, controlling heart. And that anger caused him to chase after David for years, determined to kill him. David had to hide in caves to escape the anger of Saul.

Sin in our lives can definitely make us angry.

And so, of course, can the sin of others—especially their offenses against us and those we love. Anger at offense is perhaps the most common form of anger. It's the anger we feel when someone cuts us off in traffic or keeps us waiting for an appointment or spreads rumors behind our backs. This kind of anger can be simple and easily dismissed, especially if the offense is minor. But it can also be profound, growing out of true injury and deep hurt.

We see this often in the Bible and especially clearly in the lives of Esau and Jacob. These famous twins had been in battle from the time they were in the womb. Then, as a young man,

Jacob did something horrible. Unthinkable. He stole his brother Esau's blessing.

In the Old Testament, firstborns like Esau received a double blessing. Everyone wanted to be the firstborn. Jacob had even held on to Esau's heel as they came out of the womb. Then he bought Esau's birthright. On top of that, he took advantage of his father's poor eyesight, pretended to be Esau, and stole Esau's blessing.

Needless to say, Esau was furious when he found out. Genesis 27:41 says he "seethed in anger." He said, "The time for mourning my father's death is close. And then I'll kill my brother Jacob" (*The Message*).

Offenses can definitely make us angry.

And sometimes, to be honest, we're just angry at how God seems to be handling the universe. He didn't heal the way we thought he should. He didn't give us the promotion we thought we should get. He didn't help our child the way we thought he should. He didn't let that great guy or girl we were dating stay around long enough to "put a ring on it." He didn't deal with that person who offended us, hurt us, or betrayed us the way we thought he should have.

I've come to believe, in fact, that anger at God is a big component of most angry hearts.

That's not to say that *all* anger is anger at God. When Philly told me about his angry heart in the closet that day, he was mad at a specific person and the way that person had handled his heart. My friend who e-mailed me about teaching on the angry heart was mad about something that had happened to her and at the people who had made it happen, but she was on pretty good terms with God.

But when an angry person is really shut down to a place of chronic anger that reveals itself through bitterness or revenge, it's a pretty good bet that person is angry with God. Why would God let us encounter disappointment? Why would God allow us to struggle with tormenting sin? Why would God let people get away with hurting us or others or allow people to suffer in any way?

I remember a time when I finally confronted my anger with God. If you had told me years before that I could possibly be angry with God, I would have said you'd thrown your brain over the fence. (Got that line from my sweet Nashville mom, Packer.) But then came the day when I stood in the room over my garage, phone in my hand, realizing that my (first) marriage was not going to be saved. I had just received news that left me scared and angry. And the minute I pressed End on that call, I threw the phone across the room and began to scream. The screams were so loud and the wails so deep that I couldn't remain standing. I fell to the carpet and began to beat the floor with my fists. Everything my life was supposed to be, everything I'd believed it would be, everything I'd thought God promised it would be had vanished. I felt punked, set up. I was beside myself with rage—and it was all directed straight at God.

About a month later the same scenario played out again. This time I was in a car traveling on a book tour. Events were unfolding quickly. My attorney was already working on divorce papers. I was simply trying to figure out how to get through the day without collapsing. In that little rental vehicle, I began to rant and wail to the heavens. "Why don't you fix this? You can do anything! You're God! How did you let this happen? Where have you been? Why do you let people suffer? Why don't you just come down here and make this all better?"

And then I knew. Just as the curtain was pulled back and the Wizard of Oz exposed as a fraud, my heart was exposed for what it was. All the years of rejection and disappointment and heartache and fear had created one angry heart. My body heaved from the pain of this torment.

In the middle of the groanings, God spoke. He hadn't spoken the first time—or at least I hadn't heard him. But I heard him this time. *Baby girl, I didn't make this brokenness happen. It happened because of sin, which is the result of a fallen world. But what I did was give gifts and talents and opportunities right in the middle of all the brokenness. I won't make you or anyone else choose them.*

And in that moment I knew. I had a choice of whether I would walk in this truth that God was offering me or keep my heart shut down in anger, believing the lie that the enemy of my soul was telling.

The Lie of the Angry Heart: "God Isn't Just"

What was that lie? It was the one that creates so many angry hearts: *God isn't just.*

Angry hearts feel that God doesn't shell out justice the way we would. If God were just, child abusers would always be caught and always get the ultimate penalty. If God were just, spouses who betray would never get the joy of knowing happiness again. If God were just, people who have experienced abuse would at least not have to suffer from the aftermath of that abuse.

Note the difference here between this lie and that of the disappointed heart.

The disappointed heart is dejected or let down because "God is not *for* me" or even because "life isn't fair."

But the angry heart feels strongly that action is required. It's a fight response, remember. The assumption is that someone needs to *do* something—and God's not stepping up to the plate. He's not protecting those who need to be protected. He's letting injustice prevail. He's not righting wrongs or fighting for what's right. Many people will go from there to control, assuming that "God's not doing it . . . so *I* have to!"

The lie that God is not just has caused so many people to give up on faith in God and Jesus Christ. The story of how iconic Apple founder Steve Jobs lost his faith is told in his biography:

> Even though they were not fervent about their faith, Jobs's parents wanted him to have a religious upbringing, so they took him to the Lutheran church most Sundays. That came to an end when he was thirteen. In July 1968 *Life* magazine published a shocking cover showing a pair of starving children in Biafra. Jobs took it to Sunday school and confronted the church's pastor. "If I raise my finger, will God know which one I'm going to raise even before I do it?"
>
> The pastor answered, "Yes, God knows everything."
>
> Jobs then pulled out the *Life* cover and asked, "Well, does God know about this and what's going to happen to those children?"
>
> "Steve, I know you don't understand, but yes, God knows about that."
>
> Jobs announced that he didn't want to have anything to do with worshipping such a God, and he never went back to church.[2]

You can see where he was coming from, can't you? If God exists and is doing his job, then how can there be evil in the world? Why does he let injustice happen? Maybe it's all his fault anyway! It's an easy jump from there to rejecting God outright or just living in a state of simmering resentment—with an angry heart.

Anger over perceived injustice was Adam's cry to God after his sin—our first glimpse at anger in the world.

God asks him, "Where are you?"

Adam tells him. "Um . . . well, I heard you in the garden, and I was naked, so I hid."

God has more questions: "Who told you that you were naked? Did you eat from the tree that I told you not to eat from?"

And here it comes. We're about to get to the root of it. *The Message* translation captures Adam's indignation so well: "The Woman *you* gave me as a companion, she gave me fruit from the tree, and, yes, I ate it" (Genesis 3:12, emphasis added).

See, God? At the end of the day, it is all your fault! If you hadn't given me this woman, we wouldn't be in this pickle. If you hadn't done _____, then _____ wouldn't have happened.

Sound familiar? How many times have we seen or experienced something that felt like injustice and found ourselves angry at God as a result?

The anger in an angry heart feeds on a half-truth. It recognizes that the world is all messed up—and it is. After all, this is a world where innocent babies starve to death. Where disturbed young people shoot up schools and theaters. Where wars rage through generation after generation. Where ordinary people treat even their loved ones in the most cruel ways imaginable. Where everybody suffers and eventually dies, no matter how good or bad they are. It doesn't take much discernment to understand that not all is right in our world.

But our anger turns into an angry heart when it assumes God is to blame for all this wrongness and injustice. The world is unjust because God is unjust. The world is cruel because God is cruel—or absent.

But as Deuteronomy 32:1-4 proclaims, nothing could be further from the truth.

> Listen, Heavens, I have something to tell you.
> Attention, Earth, I've got a mouth full of words.
> My teaching, let it fall like a gentle rain,
>   my words arrive like morning dew,
> Like a sprinkling rain on new grass,
>   like spring showers on the garden.
> For it's GOD's Name I'm preaching—
>   respond to the greatness of our God!
> The Rock: His works are perfect,
>   and the way he works is fair and just (*The Message*).

That's the truth to counter Satan's lies and pour cool rain on the heat of our anger. God is and always has been perfectly good and loving and just. The issue of whether or not God is just is taken out of the equation when we align our faith with the truth of the Bible.

So why is there so much injustice in the world? Because our perfectly just God loved us human beings enough to give us choice, and that choice and the resulting sin are what messed up the world. All the evils on earth that incite our anger exist because of human sin, not because of God's injustice.

Reclaiming the Angry Heart

Over the last few years I have faced a recurring challenge to keep my heart from becoming one of these angry hearts. That's because I've experienced injustice firsthand. I've watched it saddle up and try to make my front porch banister its hitching post. And there have been times in the middle of it all when I wondered how God could allow it. How can innocent people be so heartbreakingly mistreated or, worse yet, not even noticed?

Our hearts, remember, are where the enemy wages his greatest war. They are his ultimate spoil, and capturing them is his diligent quest. A few years ago he came at mine with a dagger that pierced through me. The anger that wound generated was so great that I wanted to withdraw completely. One morning I did just that. I dropped my kids off at school, came home, and climbed back in bed.

Now you need to understand: I *never* return to bed once I've gotten up. I may take a twenty-minute power nap on the sofa after lunch, but I never get back in bed. But this day I did. The anger was so great, the injustice so profound, the impact on my heart so devastating that I just wanted to get away from it all—Philly, the kids, ministry, even God.

I lay there for a long time, practically paralyzed with pain and fury. But finally, as I pulled out yet another tissue and blew my nose, I remembered something a good friend had said to me years before: "It is time to buck up!"

And that's what I heard that day from the Lord: *It is time to buck up.*

Was this anger wrong?

You bet your Nashville boots it was wrong.

Was lying there going to make it better?

No, though it made me feel better.

Would stewing over it change the situation?

No. And I didn't like what it did to my insides.

Would ignoring the situation change anything?

It never had in the past.

Then buck up and face it. Face it with me.

So what could I do? I turned to that same process of

recognition, repentance, and reflection that we've seen in other chapters, but with a slightly different spin.

It wasn't hard for me to recognize I was angry at that moment. (It isn't always quite that clear to me.) But I still needed to get honest with God and myself about what was going on. So I went upstairs to my little boy's room, where I often like to pray when it is too cold to walk outside, and began to tell God everything I was feeling—the hurt, the fear, the disappointment, but especially the anger. I was so angry.

Do you know what God did in response? Nothing like what I used to think he would do. There was no lightning bolt. He didn't scream down from his throne and say, "How dare you do anything but praise me!"

No, it was like he pulled up a chair at the table over a batch of hot biscuits and said, "Okay, let's talk. I'm listening." And he gave me the freedom to be honest. I wasn't disrespectful. I wasn't even demanding. I was simply broken—and desperate to understand what my heart felt was such extreme injustice.

Reclaiming the angry heart begins by giving ourselves the freedom to be angry. Remember, feeling anger is not a sin. Feeling anger is an unavoidable human response to a perceived threat. So it's okay to feel angry.

Our responsibility is to refuse to let the anger settle in us. It can be felt for what it is, but it cannot be lived in. Because that is when we move from understandable or inevitable anger to the choice of an angry heart. Ephesians spells this out specifically: "Go ahead and be angry. You do well to be angry—but don't use your anger as fuel for revenge. And don't stay angry" (4:26, *The Message*). When anger pushes us to lashing out or pulling in, hurting others and ourselves, then we can rest assured that sin is crouching at our door. We must master it. Because God has not given us permission to stay in our anger.

A Psalm for My Anger

Even as I sat there pouring out my anger to God, I was aware I didn't need to stay in that angry place, so I prepared to move into my regular prayer time. That's when I realized it was Thursday. Thursdays are when I typically spend my prayer time praising God. And my praise habit turned out to be a special blessing that morning because praise is a terrific antidote for anger. When we're praising God for all he is and all he does, it is hard to stay angry at him for what we are going through.

You see, the enemy loves to get us focused on what we think God is *not* doing or how we think he is *not* working on our behalf. And I realized that was what the enemy was doing to me. He was trying to get me to doubt all that God had done and all the promises God had given me in the past, in order to make me angry about what was happening now and fearful of what the future held.

And so I went to his Word. Because as we've said, spending time in the Word is the only way to combat the lies that shut down our hearts. When we remind ourselves of who God is and what he has been to us and done for us, the enemy loses his ability to get us to see God in any other light than faithful or good or just.

I picked up my Bible to read my psalm for that day. This is what it said:

Oh come, let us sing to the LORD!
Let us shout joyfully to the Rock of our salvation.
Let us come before His presence with thanksgiving;
Let us shout joyfully to Him with psalms.
For the LORD is the great God,
And the great King above all gods.
In His hand are the deep places of the earth;

181

The heights of the hills are His also.
The sea is His, for He made it;
And His hands formed the dry land.

PSALM 95:1-5

Just what I needed! God was reminding me so sweetly that he has me—no matter what. If he's got all of that under control, in his hands, he's got me too.

And if someone I love is treated unjustly, he's got him or her too.

Let It Out

Spending time in praise and in the Word helped me begin to move out of my crippling anger that morning. But I have found it also helps to take things a step further and get my anger out in other productive ways. Journaling my anger, for instance, really helps. So when I finished my prayer time that morning, I went straight to my computer and started typing in my journal.

Many other people I know have found this practice of journaling invaluable in dealing with their anger as well as with disappointment, fears, or any moment of their journey. You don't need a computer, of course, for journaling. Old-fashioned pen and paper work fine. (Just ask my dad, who wrote his sermons in longhand for forty years.) The point is to get the anger out of our heads.

It doesn't need to be in a journal either. There are many other ways to express your anger in a productive way. Here are a few ideas people have shared with me:

◆ Vent your feelings with a trusted counselor or friend.
   Make sure the person understands you're simply trying

to vent and you don't want him or her to do anything but listen. (And if you're that friend, don't feel as if you need to fix it or have answers.)

◆ Write an angry letter to a parent, a spouse or ex-spouse, a teacher or mentor, or an abuser. The letter may never be sent. In fact, it's best *not* to send it as it first comes out. There might be a time later when an edited version of the letter could be appropriate. Or it might be better to burn or erase the letter after it's written. By then it will have served its purpose of getting the anger out of you and onto the page.

◆ Make a list of fifty things you are angry about regarding your divorce, your foreclosure, your unfulfilled dream, or the future your child seems to be forfeiting.

◆ Turn the anger into art. If you paint, spend some time splashing bold colors on canvas. If you sing, pour your heart out in a song.

◆ Walk, run, ride, or dance. Anger is energy, remember, and that energy can be softened and redirected into physical activity.

I've learned that the act of letting my anger out releases the enemy's hold on me. Even as I talk or sing or type, I often start seeing things differently. I begin to see how I am contributing to the problem. I become aware of the faulty thinking about God or others that has fueled my feelings. Or I just begin to feel calmer and more rational.

We easily see the three Rs at work here. Praise, reading Scripture, and getting the anger out in positive ways are all elements of reflection, and reflection is a powerful weapon against the enemy. But the process of handling anger doesn't stop there. Next comes the repentance—or turning the anger around.

For me, this involves focusing the blame on the real source of the trouble.

Don't get confused, by the way, because I've listed reflection here as coming *before* repentance. Until now I've listed these elements in a specific order for simplicity's sake. But reclaiming a heart is rarely a simple matter, and the steps rarely happen in one-two-three order. Sometimes a fair amount of reflection is needed before we can even recognize a problem, much less repent of it. Sometimes reflection after recognition and repentance will lead us to recognize a deeper level of sin or dysfunction, and we'll need to repent again. Reflection may be required after a problem is recognized to make repentance possible. The fight to reclaim our hearts requires a constant process of recognizing, repenting, and reflecting.

The Real Enemy

I find it interesting to see what Eve did when God discovered her sin. Remember, Adam reacted with anger at her and God. He pointed the finger at both of them in blame. But Eve didn't do anything like that.

She could have pointed her finger at Adam. After all, she came from his rib. Shouldn't he have protected her, been the man of the house? But she didn't place the blame on Adam or even on God. She didn't say, "If you hadn't gone and made snakes, we wouldn't be in this pickle in the first place, now would we?" No, she pointed the finger at the original culprit: "The serpent deceived me. . . . That's why I ate it" (Genesis 3:13, NLT).

That's it exactly! Ultimately the enemy is behind all our anger, our sin, the threats to our well-being, and injustice. Ephesians 6:12 spells this out for us: "For we do not wrestle against flesh and blood, but against principalities, against powers, against the rulers of the darkness of this age, against spiritual hosts of wickedness in the heavenly places."

I'm not saying we're not responsible for our choices or that we shouldn't hold others responsible. (Eve was absolutely responsible for her choice too.) But we still need to recognize who's behind all the trouble in the world—the one who is most deserving of our anger.

When other people hurt us, it is because they are listening to the enemy of their hearts. When injustice and cruelty and death cast shadows on our lives, it's because of the Fall he initiated. He is the ultimate enemy, even if he uses another person or a circumstance against us. So he's the one we need to be angry with. We need to focus our fury on what we've allowed the thief to rob from us in our anger.

In the words of Ephesians 4:27, we must make sure we "don't give the Devil that kind of foothold" in our lives (*The Message*). The anger we hold on to gives the enemy that foothold, and trust me, once he starts, he won't stop. He will find one excuse after another to get his foot in the door of our hearts. He will rob us of our joy. He will rob our relationships of trust and intimacy. And he will rob us of our ability to be present in our lives.

That's a big one for me. When I am angry, I am not emotionally or mentally present with the people around me. Isn't that true for you too? Think of all the wonderful things you have missed because of your anger. And until we get mad at the enemy for what he is robbing from us, we won't do anything about it. We will continue to let our anger suck the life out of our hearts. But isn't it bad enough that whatever has made us angry has been done at all? Why allow anger to continue to rob from us and those we love?

So oddly enough, I think we need to handle our anger by

getting really mad—at the one who actually deserves it. We must use that angry energy to fight for our freedom, and that isn't an easy battle. For me, at least, it's a constant battle not to hand over my heart in my anger or disappointment.

Believe me, I get opportunities to practice over and over. One came the other night—again, with one of the kids. I'm talking about an every-blood-vessel-in-the-face-popping-out moment. But I knew I had a choice. I could run to the closet one more time and let Philly handle the situation. But if I did that, I knew there would be no conversation at the dinner table, no bedtime stories, no laughter at something ridiculous my husband would do.

What did I do? I tried to focus on the real source of the trouble. I reminded myself that the enemy is after my heart and will often use my closest relationships to get at me. So I chose to take a great big breath and put my anger away and to react differently. And that's what I think we need to do over and over when our natural, unavoidable anger begins to rob us of joy and threaten our hearts.

Letting Go

Sometimes letting go of anger feels impossible—although it's a lot easier if I've gone through the process of honesty, praise, reflecting on Scripture, and getting the anger out. For me, what I have found to be the greatest weapon against allowing my heart to shut down in anger—especially if it is over something someone has done—is to pray for the person who offended me. Not praying over how I feel—I covered that earlier—but intentional prayer on behalf of the person who has wounded me.

Praying for someone who has hurt me makes a huge difference because it softens my heart. It allows me to focus on who the real enemy is and to get to a place of forgiveness much more quickly. And forgiveness is crucial because maintaining a heart of unforgiveness toward someone is a cancer. It slowly eats away at the spirit, leaving devastation in its path.

Is praying for those who have hurt you and forgiving them fun?

Usually not. It's not easy, and it's rarely a one-time proposition. Chances are we'll find ourselves having to forgive the same person again and again, either for the same offense or a new one. Jesus told Peter he'd have to forgive "seventy times seven" (Matthew 18:22). Peter wanted a quick fix, a low number, a line where he could finally let go of worrying about the need to forgive and indulge himself in his anger.

But Jesus didn't offer him that. He offered him a number that represented unlimited forgiveness—because Jesus knew that continual forgiveness was the only way to protect Peter's heart from shutting down in anger.

It's always about our hearts, remember—our precious hearts. That's why the Bible urges, "Don't go to bed angry. . . . Make a clean break with all cutting, backbiting, profane talk. Be gentle with one another, sensitive. Forgive one another as quickly and thoroughly as God in Christ forgave you" (Ephesians 4:26, 31-32, *The Message*).

Does that mean we don't acknowledge wrong done to us? No.

Does it mean there won't be consequences for the wrong or justice for the injustice?

Again, no, although we might not be the one to impose the consequences or choose what form they take.

Does letting go of our anger mean we condone what was done?

Absolutely not. Nor does it mean it won't happen again or that we should automatically trust the person who has hurt us.

As Rick Warren advises, "Trust must be rebuilt over time. Trust requires a track record."[3]

But what it does mean is we get our anger directed where it belongs—at the enemy who is the real thief—and our trust in the place where *it* belongs—in our heavenly Father who is supremely confident in doing his job.

Here is the beautiful truth: we can be confident that God will avenge all wrong. He will settle scores. He will vindicate. He may not do it the way we want him to do it or in the time frame we want him to do it in. But we can trust that if we don't harden our hearts, if we keep them pure before him and continue to walk in forgiveness even when we don't want to, if we continue to do all of this, he will avenge every wrong done to us and to those we love. Truth will eventually win out. As the book of Proverbs reminds us, "Do not say, 'I'll pay you back for this wrong!' Wait for the LORD, and he will avenge you" (20:22, NIV).

My heart finally found a resting place later that stay-in-bed morning. Not only did I get out of bed, but I ended up praying for the person who had precipitated the incident. What I noticed as I prepared to teach this lesson was how often the enemy tries to get me back into the snare of anger. The event that doesn't go my way. The compliment I don't receive. The brush-off that hurts my heart. The truth is, the enemy will never stop.

Are there times I long for a break from all that hurt? Sure. But peaceful waters and days without conflict don't necessarily provide the rest we seek.

I remember once hearing somebody say that no season of our lives will be without both joy and pain. That some days may be mostly joyful, but a tinge of pain will still color the joy. And that some days may seem full of pain, but joy can be found even in the midst of the suffering. I have come to believe that is true. As long as we live, we'll never experience unmixed peace and joy.

Kind of makes you long for Eden, doesn't it? Why wouldn't we feel that way? Eden was what we were created for.

The good news is that Eden is coming back again for us—in the form of a new heaven and a new earth. When it does, every injustice ever done will be righted. Every act of cruelty will be redeemed. Death and sickness and infirmity will be banished.

And what we can be most thankful for is that the justice we *deserve*—justice for our damaged, broken, sinful, only partially reclaimed lives—will not be the justice we *receive*. Jesus stepped into our place for that.

Whenever we can grant such grace to another, we take a big step toward reclaiming our angry hearts.

CHAPTER TEN

THE FEARFUL HEART

To fear is one thing. To let fear grab you by the
tail and swing you around is another.
KATHERINE PATERSON

WE HAD JUST FINISHED the lesson on the angry heart. I was standing on the stage packing up my notes and Bible when she walked up. "It's me," she said. "It's all me. Everything you taught is all me. I'm so angry."

I knew she was angry. In fact, our conversation over lunch the week before had been one of the confirmations that I was to teach on the angry heart. So something told me she needed me to listen now. I put my stuff down as her words poured out.

It had been a tough season for this friend. Disappointment after disappointment had left her feeling dejected and angry. And when she finally took a breath, her shoulders slumped.

"You know what?" she said after a pause. "I think I'm just afraid."

That's when I heard that familiar *ding-ding* in my heart. It's the sound I'd heard throughout this journey as I listened for where we were to go next. I'm not sure what my friend said after that because I had already begun my internal argument with the Lord over whether I would heed that ding. I was really set on teaching the rescuing heart.

By the time I was driving home, I had already given in. I knew fear was where we were going. And as I quit arguing and started listening, I realized that all the other hearts I'd wanted to teach—people pleasing, rescuing, hovering—fit beautifully inside this one. So God was actually allowing me to cover everything I desired to.

I had asked my friend to write about her struggle with fear so I would have something to work with. Her e-mail was waiting for me when I got home that day:

> My husband and I both have realized we deal with
> a lot of fear in the area of money. Fear has kept us
> from saving, setting financial goals, being disciplined
> with budgeting. . . . Fear has robbed us in so many
> ways. The lie for us is that God wants to punish us
> for some reason. For me, I always had an unhealthy
> fear of my dad. He was an angry man during most
> of my formative years. Somehow I equated God with
> my dad, so in my mind God was waiting to punish
> me if I did something wrong. Looking back, even
> my decision to accept Jesus as my Savior was based
> on fear.

Sound familiar? It did to me. The specifics may vary, but I'm convinced that fear drives us to a greater extent than most of us would like to admit.

Origins of the Fearful Heart

Have you ever spent time with a little boy? They absolutely crack me up. I met one the other night at the ballpark. He was about three. And that kid wasn't afraid of anything. I mean, he was the most rough-and-tumble, full-throttle little guy I'd ever encountered. He loved to come up to our girls and say, "You stinky girl." He scrunched up his face as he said it, and then he was off to conquer a dirt pile. I loved it.

There's this wonderful sense of abandonment in the heart of a child who doesn't yet have the entrenched fears that life experience can induce. As parents, we rejoice in this—and worry about it because the world can be a dangerous place. That is why we work to instill a healthy fear in our children:

- ◆ "Don't touch that stove; you'll get burned."
- ◆ "Don't talk to strangers; they're not all friendly."
- ◆ "Don't go out without sunscreen."

These are all legitimate warnings, meant to induce a healthy fear of real threats. Usually such parental warnings help children grow up into safe, happy, reasonably cautious adults, not fearful ones. Usually—but not always. Which raises the question: How do we go from such healthy fear to a fearful heart?

It often does begin in childhood—or even before birth. According to child psychologist Tamar Chansky, studies have found evidence for "the genetic transmission of anxiety."[1] Some children come into this world with anxious or reactive temperaments. And unlike the fearless dirt-pile climber I met at the ballpark, these natural worriers may find that fear comes easily. For imaginative children especially, a shadow in the closet becomes the next monster, or the hallway becomes the place where the bogeyman might travel.

On top of this, parental anxiety can transmit itself to kids. For instance, even those legitimate "be careful" warnings, delivered too often and too tensely, can create the sense that the world is a fearful place and can teach children to be afraid. Criticism, rejection, and perpetual conflict can make a home feel unsafe and increase anxiety in children.

And sadly, of course, for some children the bogeyman is real. The awful truth is that things do happen to children. The experience of physical, emotional, or sexual abuse can easily produce a fearful adult. So can car accidents, grief and loss, or other painful experiences at a young age.

Adult experience, too, contributes to a sense of fear. My friend at the Bible study became fearful because of her history of disappointment and broken trust. She and her husband tried and failed. Then they tried again, and that failed too. They trusted people who failed them. They opened their hearts and were hurt. They opened their hearts again and were wounded. They opened their hearts yet again and were crushed. Now they can't bear the thought of opening up. The fear of another wound, another dagger, another tear is just too great. They can't bring themselves to risk it.

But not all fears can be chalked up to direct experience. Some fears are instilled in us by the warped philosophy of our culture or our religion. My friend's e-mail to me alluded to this:

> My experiences with beauty pageants really screwed me up in my teenage years and my early twenties. I always worked hard to be the best, even going as far as to abuse my body with exercise and laxatives. I ultimately feared I didn't have a good enough body, so I had to change it into what some judge or trainer thought I should look like. I thought that in order to be loved,

I had to be the best and be the first choice. . . . I have
spent a lot of my life trying to win God's love and have
felt many times that I missed the mark. Oh, that I
could just rest in the truth that he loves me as I am and
thinks I am a winner.

The fear-inducing messages vary in their wording, but not
in their effect. And so people with these beautiful, alive hearts
who once were princesses in the imaginary lands of their back-
yards and warriors of great and mighty battles on dirt piles at
the local ballpark are gradually reduced to cowering children
sleeping with the hall light on. These painful places can leave
us with hearts that are slaves to fear.

Many Expressions of Fear

Fear can show itself in our lives directly as nervousness, anxiety, worry, and panic. In extreme cases, a fear may take the
form of a phobia—an intense aversion to particular objects or
situations. The list of possible fears ranges from very specific
(lightning, spiders) to very vague and general ("what might happen"). It can involve threats from other people (strangers, even)
or just ourselves (failure). And though what is feared varies, the
experience of fear is universal—because everyone is afraid of
something.

Some of us find that fear freezes us in place, unable to make
decisions or handle uncomfortable situations. The very thought
of failing or doing something wrong can literally paralyze us.
But fear can also cause us to flee, literally or figuratively, to get
out of situations that seem threatening to us.

Fearful people may hide like Adam and Eve did in the
Garden, holing up at home instead of getting out and risk-
ing relationship. They may hide out in entertainment or

hobbies—TV, video games, books, movies, sports. Some disappear into addictions—the images on the computer screen,
the alcohol hidden in the closet, the obsessive shopping trips—
while others simply disappear altogether. "See ya later!" they say
as their feet cross the threshold of the door. "I'm outta here."
And they are.

Even worthwhile activities can easily become places where
we hide from what we fear. I often do this at times when I
should be working on a book or a lesson. When faced with that
looming blank screen—and any writer or teacher will tell you
that can be a terrifying prospect—I'll end up checking e-mail,
cleaning my desk, or straightening my closet, anything to hide
from the fear of not having something fresh to say. If I'm really
desperate, I'll clean out the fridge!

Freezing in place or running and hiding are perhaps the
most overt expressions of fear in our lives. But fear can also
show itself in more subtle forms.

Some fearful people, for example, become *people pleasers*.
They always say the right thing. They're usually the first to volunteer. They're often very popular and helpful. But dig down
a little deeper and you'll find an insecure person. Instead of
operating out of a real heart of service or a hospitable spirit,
people pleasers operate out of a need to be okay with everyone.

People pleasers fear they won't be appreciated, liked, or
accepted. They might be talked about or even rejected. So they
go to great lengths to keep any of that from happening. They
will wear themselves out "managing" everyone's happiness.
They obsess over making sure everyone has the right seat at the
table for the holidays, that all the conversation is distributed
evenly, that they haven't turned their backs on anyone for too
long. They may study a room—the expressions, the unspoken
words—to be sure no one is upset. They will sacrifice their own

desires and opinions to those of their spouses, their children, their bosses, or their friends in order to keep the peace, even at the cost of their own hearts.

And that, my friend, is exactly what is at stake. Because what are people pleasers really doing? They are taking God off the throne of their hearts and placing other people there. They're like the people in Jesus' day who "loved to please men more than they desired to glorify God" (John 12:43, *The Voice*).

Rescuing is another fear-based behavior. Rescuers take on the role of damage control in the lives of people around them—usually (but not always) loved ones. When a child creates a mess, the rescuer will swoop in and clean up all the debris in hopes that no one will ever notice what happened. When a girlfriend gets into trouble, the rescuer will step in and take care of it. When a spouse takes on more than he or she can handle (or wants to handle), the rescuer will take on part of the load. And while the rescuer may claim to do this out of love, the primary motivation is fear. Rescuers rescue because they fear the consequences of the other person's actions will bring them pain as well—and they are desperately afraid of feeling that pain.

Say, for example, that a man knows his wife's spending is out of control. Instead of letting her (and himself) experience the consequences of that spending—the repossessed car, the lost home—the husband swoops in and gets another job. Why? Because if he lets her suffer the consequences, he'll suffer them as well. It seems easier to become rescuer, savior, fixer, or enabler.

Or perhaps a young woman copes with her boyfriend's anger by defending him, admonishing others, even taking the blame—all in an attempt to divert where the real blame should lie: on the one who lacks the self-control to deal with his own heart. She thinks she's doing this to protect him, but she's really doing it to protect herself from his anger and its possible consequences.

Parents can easily move into the rescuer mode, stepping in to protect their young children, teenagers, or even adult children from the consequences of their actions. It can start with delivering forgotten lunch money and homework to school and move on to paying fines, floating loans, or even posting bail. The conscious motive may be love and protection, but such rescuing is usually based on fear of what might happen if the child is allowed to fail—and the discomfort the parent might feel as a result.

Philly recently encountered this rescuing urge with one of our kids. Sports have always been a huge thing in the Jones household, with Philly's dad a football coach, his mom working for years with Fellowship of Christian Athletes, and Philly's own years of playing football. As a result, Philly loves almost any kind of sport, and he loves coaching too. He has coached our children's sports teams for years because he enjoys it so much and also because it affords him more time with them.

Not long ago, however, Philly gave up coaching a team one of the kids play on. He transitioned to simply being a dad on the sideline. This proved incredibly difficult for him. If that child made a mistake, Philly wasn't able to step in and help. He couldn't fix the mistake or adjust for it as he had been able to when he was coaching. He had to watch as his child suffered the consequences.

Later Philly and I sat in Ken's office and talked about the pain of this circumstance. Philly expressed his shock at how painful it was. But he knew it was time for him to let go, that the lesson of making it without being rescued could set that child up for wonderful things down the road. I think Philly also had to come to grips with his intense desire for his kid to be the best on the field and learn how to handle himself when that child wasn't. Letting go of his rescuing tendencies was a definite challenge, but we're both glad he chose to face it.

Like people pleasers, rescuers often let their fears confuse them about who plays the god role in their relationships. In this case, they try to take it on themselves—to become the savior in the lives of others. After all, who needs to seek the real Savior when someone else is always swooping in to save the day?

Hovering is yet another form of fear-based behavior. People who have grown up with deep insecurities or painful loss are prime candidates for hovering because their fear of further loss is so deep.

A hoverer will smother a friendship, for example, calling too often, demanding too much, being both overgenerous and much too needy. They desire that the friend be their "best" or even their "only."

Spouses can be hoverers as well, nervously watching for any sign of unhappiness in the marriage, catering to a mate's every whim to keep him or her "happy," worrying whenever the husband or wife tries to do anything separate. Like the hovering friend, the hovering spouse is terrified of losing control and also losing the relationship. Sadly, when they hover too close, they put themselves in danger of the very thing they fear.

Hovering parents are so common they've been honored with a special name: "helicopter parents." Coined in the mid-1980s or early 1990s, this term describes a parent who perpetually checks, rechecks, interferes, manipulates, or does everything for their children instead of allowing them the freedom to grow and thrive.[2] (As you might guess, hovering parents very easily become rescuers for their children.)

And then there are those whose fear spurs them to fight. This can take the form of an aggressive reaction—like the child of a friend who described herself perceptively as a "fear biter." Like a dog who snaps when it feels threatened, she was likely to overreact to being teased or threatened by lashing out physically or verbally.

But "fear fighting" can also involve fighting *for* something. This is what the friend I introduced at the beginning of this chapter tends to do. She is a roll-up-her-sleeves, fight-to-the-death kind of person. She can fight with her words or with her actions. If it looks like something she cares about is going to be lost, she digs in her heels and figures out how to save it. For people like her, combative fear can easily turn into rescuing behavior or anger.

I see people fight for all kinds of things. I watched one man battle desperately to make it in the music industry, terrified that without it he would be seen as a failure. Sadly, his relentless fight cost him everything—his family, his dream, and most of his friends.

I watched a young woman fight hard for a young man she wanted to marry. Spurred by fear that he would get away and no one else would come along, she put all her energy into "landing" him—and she finally did it. But her first years of marriage have been brutal. Wounding words between them have left scars that may never completely heal. From my perspective, much of the conflict can be traced back to her initial pursuit of him. Because fighting from a place of fear never leaves room for God, even victories become tainted.

The Sin of a Fearful Heart

Did you know fear entered this world at the Fall?

Think about it. What was the first thing Adam and Eve did after they ate the fruit? They hid. They covered their physical bodies with fig leaves, and then they tried to avoid God. When God asked Adam, "Where are you?" Adam's response was "I heard you walking in the garden, so I hid. I was *afraid* because I was naked" (Genesis 3:9-10, NLT, emphasis added).

Immediately after that, Adam fought God with his accusing words: "The woman you gave me . . ." (v. 12, NLT).

From the beginning, in other words, fear has walked hand in hand with sin. And from the beginning, God and fear have been at odds. Look at how God treated Adam and Eve.

First, God obviously didn't feel compelled to please Adam and Eve at all costs. Yes, he delighted in giving them a garden for their pleasure, but he also had no problem with forbidding them from eating of one of the trees. Even before the Fall, his ultimate concern was not their pleasure, but the state of their hearts.

Second, God didn't jump into rescue mode when Adam and Eve were in danger of sinning. He didn't interfere when Eve talked to the serpent or swoop in and pull the fruit from her hands. And after it was all done, he didn't spare the man and woman from the consequences of their actions. Instead, he set into motion a place for redeeming the entire situation.

Third, he didn't hover over them—at least not in the sense that helicopter parents hover over their offspring. He didn't zoom in whenever they were at risk of stumbling or eating from the wrong tree. Instead, he set boundaries, lavished them with an indescribable love, provided them with everything needed for their success, then released them to make their own choices.

Can you see what I'm getting at here? There was nothing fear based in the way God treated Adam and Eve.

The fear had everything to do with their sin.

That's not to say that fear is *always* a sin. Like anger, fear is a built-in human response, the "flight" part of the fight-or-flight mechanism. And as I have mentioned, healthy fear serves an important purpose. It prompts us to steer clear of danger and keeps us safe.

There's another kind of healthy fear that is the very opposite of sin. Many of us can quote Proverbs 1:7: "The fear of the LORD is the beginning of knowledge." But this kind of fear is not at all the same thing as the anxiety, worry, and dread we've been talking about. The Amplified version describes it as "the reverent and worshipful fear of the Lord." It has a lot more to do with love than with what we usually call fear.

Think of parents who "fear" hurting their child. It's not because they are afraid of their child, but because they love that little one so deeply. That is the type of fear our Father has set up as holy—fear that is really love and respect. He doesn't want us afraid of him. He wants us to walk in such deep love that we desire him above everything else and we fear anything that keeps us from living out what he has called us to live out.

Unfortunately the fear that shuts down our hearts is a completely different experience from the healthy fear we've just described. And a fearful heart is definitely a sin—for several reasons.

For one thing, entrenched or habitual fear is a form of disobedience—because God commands us *not* to fear. In fact, variations of "Don't be afraid" appear more often than any other command in the Bible.[3] I don't think God is telling us never to feel afraid. I think he's telling us to avoid letting fear take up residence in our lives. He's telling us not to have a fearful heart.

More to the point, this kind of fear is inherently incompatible with love and can cut us off from God himself. The book of 1 John tells us explicitly:

> God is love. When we take up permanent residence
> in a life of love, we live in God and God lives in us.
> This way, love has the run of the house, becomes at
> home and mature in us, so that we're free of worry on
> Judgment Day—our standing in the world is identical

with Christ's. *There is no room in love for fear.* Well-formed love banishes fear. Since fear is crippling, a fearful life—fear of death, fear of judgment—is one not yet fully formed in love.

4:17-18, *The Message* (EMPHASIS ADDED)

If God is love, and if he commands us above all to love him and love others, that doesn't leave much room for worry and anxiety to take hold. But if we let fear shut down our hearts, we're basically crowding love out of our lives—and that is undoubtedly sin.

Fear is a gripper, if you will. Fear grips the arms of seats in movie theaters. Fear grips the handle above the door in the car. Fear grips the gun when you think you hear an intruder. Fear grips your chest when you get the midnight phone call. And what gripping does is remove the ability for anything to get inside. Nothing gets inside clenched fists.

I tell our kids all the time when they're having "sharing" issues, "If you hold your hands in fists, God can't get anything inside them. But if you hold them open, God can get anything to you."

The same is true with our hearts.

The Lie of the Fearful Heart: "God Can't Be Trusted"

In a sense, fear is a "gateway sin" for many other forms of disobedience and separation from God. It underlies other kinds of shut-down hearts. And the lie behind it is just as basic: *God can't be trusted.* Once we fall for that lie, our whole world begins to look different. We start thinking we can't count on God to love us and protect us and tell us the truth and keep his promises. And when we think that way, everything we encounter feels like a threat. Fear is the inevitable result.

This lie was set up perfectly the moment Satan looked at Eve and challenged her with *"Did God really say* you must not eat the fruit . . . ?"* (Genesis 3:1, NLT, emphasis added).

Not real different from the way he strikes the chords of mistrust in our hearts today, is it?

"Did God really say . . . ?" We can fill in the blank. He sets us up with doubt about our God. One thing we can say about the enemy of our souls is that he hasn't changed his tactics much over time.

But the enemy wasn't through. After striking Eve with the venom of doubt, he followed right behind with a deadly contradiction. "You won't die!" he insisted (v. 4, NLT).

What? God said if I ate of this tree I would die. And now you're telling me it's not going to happen? If that's true, then what God has said he is, is all a big charade. How can I believe he wants what is best for me?

From the very dawn of creation, the enemy has been trying to convince humans that God can't be trusted. He did it with Eve, and he continues to do it with us. He wants us to fall for the lie that we can't depend on God

- ◆ to keep his promises;
- ◆ to keep us safe in times of threat or danger;
- ◆ to provide what we need;
- ◆ to guide us in times of confusion;
- ◆ to care for those we love; or
- ◆ to protect us from other people's poor choices.

The fact that the enemy is perpetually after our hearts with this kind of whopper—that we cannot trust the One who is most trustworthy of all—is what should really make us afraid. Very afraid.

Reclaiming the Fearful Heart

Reclaiming the fearful heart begins, as always, with recognition. And for me, recognition usually begins with asking questions about God and about my own life.

I remember sitting across from Ken one day and talking about an issue that brought me intense fear. As I unwrapped the pain of my divorce and realized all the different ways I had shut down my heart, I discovered what a huge factor fear had become in my life.

"It's interesting, Ken. When it comes to ministry, I'm not afraid of anything. If I need to confront someone I'm working with and say, 'We need to do this differently' or 'This isn't working' or 'I think we have to go another way than we originally planned,' I'm fine with that. Or if someone invites me into their world for spiritual direction or advice, I'm not afraid to speak God's truth. But when it's just about me and my heart, I'm afraid to ask for what I need."

Ken looked at me. "Why is that?"

That wasn't hard to answer. "Because ministry isn't about me. It's about God. I'm not afraid to fight for God."

"So you don't think you're worth fighting for?"

At that I stopped. Those words settled on me, and I allowed myself to sit in them for a moment. I had never thought of it that way. "I guess not."

This conversation woke me up to my heart, and I was able to recognize the particular pattern of fear that I had allowed to be created for me. I was the middle child, the typical peace-maker. Our family life hadn't always been easy, and I was the one who loved to make sure everyone smiled or felt included or valued. Yes, I grew up as a people pleaser—perhaps out of fear of being overlooked or fear of conflict.

Then, in my first marriage, I became a rescuer. On many different occasions, instead of allowing the consequences of my husband's poor choices simply to play out, I would come to the rescue. To be honest, most of my rescuing happened because the consequences would affect me as well. I didn't want to hurt, truth be told, and I resorted to rescuing out of this fear of pain.

No wonder I found myself, in the aftermath of my divorce, a prisoner of a fearful heart. I knew it was time to own up to my fearful habits, repent of my fear, and move past fear into the truth of God's Word—the truth that because my Father is so trustworthy, I don't have to be afraid.

Learning to Walk in Love

On Ken's advice, I tried to ask myself questions before I made most of my decisions, especially if I found anxiety gripping me in any form. I would ask myself, "Okay, what is my motivator here? Am I being motivated by an unhealthy fear of what might happen if I make a certain decision, or am I being motivated by what I feel that you, Father, are asking me to do? Am I living in fear or living in love?"

The difference is essential because love and fear, remember, are incompatible. Only by keeping our focus on God's trustworthy love will we ever be able to move past our fears.

Jan Meyers tells a story in *Listening to Love* about a friend of hers named Allyson. While on a business trip, Allyson received word that her son had suffered a seizure—his third in recent months. He was in no immediate danger, but Allyson still struggled with being away from her child and with trying to understand what God had for her family. She was finally able to settle her fears not by understanding, but by focusing on the trustworthiness of God's love:

As Allyson reached for the Tree of Life, its branches humbly bowed to reassure her that although much is hidden, all is well. She could have easily reached for the Tree of Knowledge of Good and Evil, trying to convince herself that she knew what God was doing or what the outcome would be. But if she had done this, she would have missed intimacy with her God. The mind of Christ allows us to choose the Tree of Life, a place of rest amid uncertainty, even though we're tempted to choose the path that requires no faith and no tension.

Love is the pulse of our faith, and it is the sap pulsing through the Tree of Life. Think of it this way: God alone held the knowledge of good and evil in the garden. He wanted us to work and play and learn of him, enjoying him. We grabbed the branches and said, "There's more!" in stubborn rebellion and fell hard as the weight of too much knowledge crashed on our hearts. Too much knowledge was *death*. . . .

When Love is the source of our religion, I can trust Jesus's intentions as the anchor for my heart.[4]

What I had done for years was to walk in fear instead of love. My stubborn rebellion had put me on the path that "requires no faith and no tension" because I didn't like tension. I liked peace. But what I had created was just a false sense of peace, because eventually something or someone would erupt.

So I had to come to a place of repentance, to change my pattern of behavior. And in asking God the question "What is my motivator?" I was also alerting my own heart to focus not on what another person might say or do or think, but instead on what my Father, the Designer and Creator of my heart, was asking me to do out of his intense love for me.

My pastor said the other day, "No demand, no expectation trumps the call of God on your life."

If I allow someone else's demands or expectations of me to move my heart to an action of fear, then I have given that other person the place of lordship in my life, and that place only belongs to One.

The One We Can Trust

Ken suggested I take the questions a step further. Because fear is ultimately related to a sense of threat, he recommended that I ask, "What is being threatened? Is it my material security? My physical security? My value? What do I need that I don't trust God to provide for me?"

Hiding or fighting usually involves a perceived threat of danger to our physical beings or to our hearts. People-pleasing behavior—saying yes too readily, taking on too much, hesitating to confront others—sometimes involves the fear that I won't be liked or loved, that others won't value me. Rescuing patterns often emerge from the threat of pain. Hovering typically involves the threat of loss but also questions of value: *Am I an adequate parent? Am I worthy of having a friend?*

So what is the antidote to all those questions of threat? The answer is settling our hearts that God can be trusted to protect us and meet our needs. Jesus spoke directly to that issue in his Sermon on the Mount:

> Therefore I tell you, stop being perpetually uneasy (anxious and worried) about your life, what you shall eat or what you shall drink; or about your body, what you shall put on. Is not life greater [in quality] than food, and the body [far above and more excellent] than clothing?

Look at the birds of the air; they neither sow nor reap nor gather into barns, and yet your heavenly Father keeps feeding them. Are you not worth much more than they?

And who of you by worrying and being anxious can add one unit of measure (cubit) to his stature or to the span of his life?

And why should you be anxious about clothes? Consider the lilies of the field and learn thoroughly how they grow; they neither toil nor spin.

Yet I tell you, even Solomon in all his magnificence (excellence, dignity, and grace) was not arrayed like one of these.

But if God so clothes the grass of the field, which today is alive and green and tomorrow is tossed into the furnace, will He not much more surely clothe you, O you of little faith?

Therefore do not worry and be anxious, saying, What are we going to have to eat? or, What are we going to have to drink? or, What are we going to have to wear?

For the Gentiles (heathen) wish for and crave and diligently seek all these things, and your heavenly Father knows well that you need them all.

But seek (aim at and strive after) first of all His kingdom and His righteousness (His way of doing and being right), and then all these things taken together will be given you besides.

So do not worry or be anxious about tomorrow, for tomorrow will have worries and anxieties of its own. Sufficient for each day is its own trouble.

MATTHEW 6:25-34, AMP

Oh, my friend, the God we serve is so loving, so capable, so concerned with the finest details of our lives. He knows exactly what we need and provides it. All we have to do is seek him, and he'll take care of the rest. And he is trustworthy in a way that no other human relationship—even the best human relationship—can be.

I remember realizing the real truth of this not long after I married Philly. That man completed so much for me. He really did. He fulfilled things inside me that I didn't think I would ever know this side of heaven. He loved me as I had never been loved, made me laugh harder than I had ever laughed, heard me in ways I had never been heard, saw me in ways I had never been seen.

When we were dating, he once told me he'd considered googling me. But then he said, "I didn't want to learn you that way. I want to *encounter* you." And he has done exactly that. He has read every book I've written and will come to me with pages dog-eared so he can ask questions about them.

And yet, I recall one night after Philly and I had this wonderful day together, when I came home feeling a sense of incompleteness. As I lay in bed in the dark, a deep sense of gratitude came over me. I began to engage my Father as the depth of my need for being known—a need that even Philly cannot fill completely—became clear.

As much as I love my husband, I go to my Father before I go to Philly. He walked me down the aisle to meet Philly, and he walks outside with me in the early morning as we talk. He hangs out with me in my car. He knows me . . . and he values me. No human, no matter how good the relationship may be, will ever value us or care for us or know us the way our heavenly Father does.

Does this mean that we will never know fear or that the things we fear will never happen? Not exactly. We still live in a fallen world, a dangerous world, and it's still possible to get hurt. But even then God has us. Did you hear me? No matter what happens to us, God has us right in the palm of his hand. We might not always understand him, but we can always trust him.

God has you and he can be trusted. Claiming that truth is the key for reclaiming the fearful heart in any of its expressions.

Notes for People Pleasers

Reclaiming this form of fearful heart begins by coming to terms with the reality that our heavenly Father values us. Our value to him is completely separate from any committee we ever chair, any meal we ever take to someone who is sick. If we can take that to heart, we don't need to base our sense of value on the opinions of others.

I have come to believe that God rarely calls us to sacrifice ourselves perpetually for others, and he never calls us to sacrifice ourselves on the altar of others' opinions. When our family or our health or our heart begins to suffer because of what we are doing, there is usually something else going on.

Sometimes reclaiming a people-pleasing heart means having difficult conversations. Sometimes it simply means saying no to someone's request. Sometimes it involves clearly stating my disagreement with someone else's observation of me or something they think I should do. Sometimes I need to go to people whose words or actions have affected me, ask them what their real intent was, and give them the opportunity to clarify.

These past three years have been full of this kind of dialogue for me. Sometimes my attempts at conversation have been met with receptive hearts, and other times they haven't. But I'm learning to trust that how other people respond is a reflection of their heart, not mine. In it all, I'm learning to trust the sturdy truth of Luke 12:4-5:

I tell you, my friends, do not be afraid of those who kill the body and after that can do no more. But I will show you whom you should fear: Fear him who, after your body has been killed, has authority to throw you into hell. Yes, I tell you, fear him (NIV).

Notes for Rescuers

One of the most powerful realities a rescuer must recognize is that love doesn't always mean immediately coming to the rescue.

Remember the story of Mary and Martha, who sent word to Jesus that their brother Lazarus was sick and about to die? What did he do? He didn't go. In fact, he didn't go for two whole days. And by the time he got there, Lazarus was dead.

I don't know where we developed the idea that loving someone always means rescuing that person. That's just not true. Not even God does that. He doesn't always answer us in the way we desire. Sometimes he lets us contend with our thorns in the flesh—the questions that can't be answered, the desires that aren't fulfilled, the pain that isn't soothed. Nor does he save us from all the consequences of our actions. And I don't believe he wants us to do that for others either.

When we surrender our hearts to rescuing others, it is as if the person has handed us their bags to carry. There we stand, our arms loaded down with someone else's bags. For some of us, it is time to let the bags fall or hand them back.

If we are always there to rescue someone from their problems or carry their bags for them, then they have no need for God. Why? Because we have taken on the role of savior. So we can't go blaming God when this person doesn't come to the realization of their need for him. Why turn to him when they have us?

It's okay not to have all the answers for someone we care about. It really is. Because our not having the answers forces others to figure out where to find them.

The truth is, none of us can save anybody else. We can love other people. We can help them—to a point. But we can't save them; God is the only Savior. We have the freedom to determine that our own heart is worth saving from the fear that drives us to rescue others.

Notes for Hoverers

A hoverer, like a rescuer, has to realize that ultimately everyone will make their own choices. Our role is simply to parent the best we can. Love our spouse the best we can. Be the best friend we can be. Love God to the best of our ability. If we've done that, then the decisions other people make are theirs, and we have to leave them in the hands of God, the ultimate protector. Instead of inserting ourselves into other people's lives, why not give those people the opportunity to engage us on their terms?

Perhaps the most painful truth that must be faced to reclaim a hovering heart is simply that hovering doesn't help anybody. It just causes more pain.

Can marriages be healed after infidelity?

Absolutely. I've seen it time and time again.

Can children who have made terrible, life-changing choices still become different people down the road?

Oh, the stories I could tell.

Do they both take work and a rebuilding of trust?

Yes, a lot of work and plenty of time.

But does consuming ourselves with fearful hovering lead to quicker or better outcomes?

Not that I've ever encountered.

What does make a difference is learning to trust. And not just learning to trust others, but learning to trust God.

Paul writes in Romans:

> I pray that God, the source of hope, will fill you completely with joy and peace because you trust in him. Then you will overflow with confident hope through the power of the Holy Spirit.
>
> ROMANS 15:13, NLT

Running with Open Hands

One of the best questions for us to ask in any fearful situation is "Am I running *to* something or *from* something?" Whenever we are running *from* something, we are headed the wrong way. We should always be running *to* something—running toward God.

In addition to running in the right direction, we have to learn to hold things loosely, to relax our hands that want to grip too tightly or clench into fists.

I remember shortly after I knew I loved Philly, there was a moment when we weren't sure if forever was what God had planned. The conversation came over our favorite meal—fajitas—at our local Mexican dive.

I knew he still had some soul-searching to do. He needed some clear direction, a sense of release before he could commit to me with a whole heart. And though I understood that on some level, my heart was frantic with fear. After we had talked awhile, I escaped to the restroom and shut myself in a stall. I wanted to cry. I wanted to run. But what I didn't want to do was hurt. I'd been there, done that, had the battle scars to prove it—and I didn't want any more. God had told me he would get his man to me, hadn't he? So why wasn't it working?

In that stall I leaned my head against the door and opened

my hands. I said, "Father, I don't know what you're doing. I don't know what you have planned, but what I do know is that no matter what, you've got me."

In that moment he brought to mind the story of Abraham and Isaac and the statement Abraham made to his traveling companions before he and Isaac headed up the mountain. He said, "We will come back" (Genesis 22:5). That was what God whispered to me, that we would be back. We might be about to climb a mountain, but we would come back down it together. But if I hadn't quieted my soul and unclenched my fists, I would have never been able to hear what he wanted to speak to me.

God's Other Reason

For years I've studied those first three chapters of Genesis. And one of the most enlightening things I've discovered in those chapters is the *other* reason I believe God removed Adam and Eve from the Garden.

Did they sin?

Yes.

Were there consequences to their sin?

Absolutely.

Was Eden changed at that moment from something beautiful to something heartbreaking?

Undeniably so.

Yet still in the middle of that mess was this loving Father. After he confronted Adam and Eve and revealed to them the consequences of their sin, he made clothes for them. How amazing is this? Remember, the critical heart would convince us that if we failed this way, God would cast us out altogether, just get rid of us. But he didn't do that. Instead, he pulled his children to him and replaced those pitiful little fig leaves with garments made by his own hands. And then, talking to the rest of the Trinity, he said:

> "Look, the human beings have become like us, knowing both good and evil. What if they reach out, take fruit from the tree of life, and eat it? Then they will live forever!" So the LORD God banished them from the Garden of Eden, and he sent Adam out to cultivate the ground from which he had been made. After sending them out, the LORD God stationed mighty cherubim to the east of the Garden of Eden. And he placed a flaming sword that flashed back and forth to guard the way to the tree of life.
>
> GENESIS 3:22-24, NLT

Can you see God's rich and deep love in all this? If you can't, look more closely.

God made us for sweet relationship with him, those face-to-face, cool-of-the-day encounters he enjoyed in the Garden. He created us for perfect fellowship with him, but our sin ruined that personal exchange.

Why? Because God had to remove us from the Garden. God knew that if he allowed us to stay in the Garden and we then ate of the tree of life, sin and separation would be our permanent state. The sicknesses our bodies endure, the disharmony and divorces our marriages suffer, the losses we have to experience, the financial crises, the societal perversions—all of that would be eternal. Our sinful state would be sealed, and our hearts would forever be separated from God, with no hope of redemption. So God in his great love removed Adam and Eve from the Garden and set angels at the gate. He did it to make sure we would not always have to endure the pain we suffer today—and that the garment of sin we enter the world wearing would be stripped away when we receive Jesus as our Savior.

It had to be done—for our sakes. But it came at the price of those in-person moments between God and humans.

I can tell you, I have some sweet moments with my Father. On our walks in the morning or when I'm lying in bed at night and the house is quiet or when I'm listening to the laughter of my bonus kids or watching the delight on my husband's face when he's coaching our son's football team, I experience God.

But there is an element of him, once known by the first humans, that I have yet to encounter. And I believe he misses that. So he set into motion the plan to once again be able to enjoy us face-to-face, a plan that began with our banishment from the Garden.

The screen saver on my computer shows a scene of two Adirondack chairs on a white beach, next to the clear blue water. I love to look at that picture because it reminds me that my Father and I will one day sit and simply enjoy each other's company. I'll sip a cold Coke, and he can have whatever it is that he enjoys.

Okay, I know that it might not be exactly as I imagine, but I know it will be good—better than I could dream. I long for that day. And I believe with all my heart that he longs for it too, even more intensely than I do. He was even willing to endure separating himself from us for a season, just so he could enjoy us for eternity.

My friends, if we can't trust a Father who will do that . . . I don't know what we can trust.

With that kind of trustworthy Father, what do we have to fear?

CHAPTER ELEVEN

THE WEARY HEART

Why, I feel all thin, sort of stretched, if you know what I
mean: like butter that has been scraped over too much bread.
That can't be right. I need a change, or something.

J. R. R. TOLKIEN

YOU KNOW YOU'RE WEARY when you're too weary to write the chapter on the weary heart. But that's where I was. There I sat in Panera Bread drinking my hot tea, eating my toast, reading my Bible. And crying.

I'd been like that for the past two weeks. I was chalking it up to being perimenopausal (which my doctor assures me I'm not), teaching a Bible study, finishing up a book by the deadline, having another book deadline right on top of that. Tack onto that my roles as wife, bonus mom, friend, counselor, grocery shopper, top chef, taxi driver, and monitor of five different e-mail accounts and two Facebook pages, and I was about ready to hit the Eject button.

I turned another page in the book of Exodus. Our church had started a new Bible reading program the first of the year, and we'd made it to chapter 18. Moses had led the children of Israel out of the desert, listened to their complaining, and begun fighting some people who had attacked them. Then his father-in-law showed up. Just what Moses needed, right? Some might say having the in-laws appear right in the middle of everything else sounds like one more thing to worry about.

But Moses' father-in-law turned out to be a treasure—as I'll explain later in this chapter. And that passage of Scripture, which I had read so many times, held a valuable new meaning for me. God used it to let me know I was close to burnout. If I was going to survive, I needed to let go of some things. But I didn't know how I could do that.

I thought of one particular commitment that was especially draining. My friend Deneen and I had been discussing it just that morning. I didn't see how I could afford to give it up, but her take was that I couldn't afford *not* to give it up. "It takes—what?—three hours, and then you need a day to recoup afterward. Why lose a whole day when you can let go of three hours? No one's soul is at stake if you give this up. But your soul—or your health—might be at stake if you keep doing it."

As I sat there pondering what I'd just read in the Bible, I realized she was right. God was speaking to me through his Word and her words. I really did need to let go.

Another thought struck me. *Maybe I should teach on the weary heart this week.* I already had a lesson prepared, but I was willing to take on another one.

No, not this week. The answer came immediately. *You are too weary.*

Why Are We So Weary?

Weariness is an epidemic. We see its residue everywhere. And it can become the state of our hearts in multiple ways.

Intense striving—for money, for possessions, for power or recognition—can certainly make us weary, and we live in a culture where striving is a way of life. Productivity amounts to an obsession in some sectors. The pressure to make more and consume more and *be* more never seems to let up. *Busy* and *frantic* often serve as bragging words. Vacations rarely last long enough for anyone to relax fully. Economic woes simply seem to add to the pressure as the drive changes from "Climb the ladder" to "Don't fall off." Although many critics have attacked the United States for its fast-paced, striving culture, other countries, such as China,[1] seem determined to jump on the bandwagon.

Striving is far from a new phenomenon. Thousands of years ago, King Solomon, wrote poignantly of the weariness that comes from striving. In the book of Proverbs, he wrote, "Weary not yourself to be rich; cease from your own [human] wisdom. Will you set your eyes upon wealth, when [suddenly] it is gone? For riches certainly make themselves wings, like an eagle that flies toward the heavens" (23:4-5, AMP).

We've felt it—those seasons when we've put in sixty- or eighty-hour weeks. That extra job we took on to pay the bills. The countless e-mails we feel the pressure to respond to, the calendar that dictates us instead of us dictating it. The perpetual need for the bigger house, the nicer car, the next new thing. The pressure of balancing work and family.

No wonder we are weary! Striving will wear us out.

And so will a prolonged period of troubles or disappointment.

Elijah learned this when he faced a series of intense attacks by Queen Jezebel. She was killing Yahweh's prophets right and left. Elijah's showdown with the prophets of the queen's god, Baal, had brought him to the queen's attention: "Ahab told Jezebel all that Elijah had done and how he had slain all the prophets [of

Baal] with the sword" (1 Kings 19:1, AMP). So Jezebel set out to kill Elijah, just as she had killed the other prophets. Elijah fled the queen, but he couldn't outrun his weariness.

David felt weariness when Saul pursued him year after year, determined to take his very life. "I am weary with my groaning," he wrote. "All night I soak my pillow with tears, I drench my couch with my weeping. My eye grows dim because of grief; it grows old because of all my enemies" (Psalm 6:6-7, AMP).

Some of us have felt the same way: sick of our groaning, crying into our pillows night after night, feeling old before our time. Perhaps we've known seasons of prolonged warfare—fighting for our marriages or the hearts of our children year after year, slogging through a health crisis that seems to drag on with no relief. We've encountered disappointment after disappointment: the futile wait for a life partner, the heartbreaking—and expensive—quest for a child, the promotions that don't materialize, the business that never makes it off the ground. Or like David, we've felt besieged by enemies who don't seem to let up.

Prolonged periods of struggle are enough to wear anybody out. But it's important to recognize that ministry can do the same.

I noticed this specifically in the life of Moses. Moses sat and judged the children of Israel from morning until evening. His ministry never seemed to let up because his people's needs didn't let up.

People in ministry know this. Pastors are on call 24-7. When I was growing up in a minister's home, it seemed like almost every family vacation would be cut short when someone in the congregation died. We used to pray for God to keep everyone alive until we could get back home!

Ministry is demanding. Needs are great—and everyone feels that his or her needs are the greatest. Wisdom and discernment are essential. But even with careful choices and prioritizing, ministry can make you weary.

Have you ever thought of sin as a wearying proposition? The prophet Jeremiah did:

> "Beware of your neighbor!
>   Don't even trust your brother!
> For brother takes advantage of brother,
>   and friend slanders friend.
> They all fool and defraud each other;
>   no one tells the truth.
> With practiced tongues they tell lies;
>   *they wear themselves out with all their sinning.*
> They pile lie upon lie
>   and utterly refuse to acknowledge me,"
>   says the LORD.
>
> JEREMIAH 9:4-6, NLT (EMPHASIS ADDED)

Sin by definition separates us from God, preventing us from experiencing the strength and refreshment of his presence. Sin is a struggle that can really beat us bloody—and absolutely wear us out.

The Lie of the Weary Heart: "God Needs Me"

When I finally got honest with myself about the pride underlying my weariness, I found myself face-to-face with the prideful lie of the weary heart: *God needs me.*

This lie convinces us that God needs us to do what we are doing, that important things just won't happen unless we step up to the plate and do them. That is the whopper the weary heart falls for every time—the lie that *makes* it weary.

- ◆ God needs me to volunteer for this activity because no one else wants to do it.
- ◆ God needs me to be in charge because no one else can do it as well.
- ◆ God needs me to minister to all of these people because, after all, they are coming to me.
- ◆ God needs me to fight this battle longer because the battle is still here.
- ◆ God needs me to work longer at my job because a lot of people don't even have jobs.
- ◆ God needs me to fight this sin that's beaten me bloody and conquer it *before* I come to him.

Do you see the pride in that—the *me, me, me* behind the earnest desire to do right? This one can be so sneaky, so seductive, especially for well-meaning, God-fearing people. It can trick us into more sin—refusing God's invitation to rest and trying to power through in our own strength, which of course makes us even more weary and shut down.

My friend, God doesn't need us now—nor has he ever needed us.

The God who made the world and everything in it
is the Lord of heaven and earth and does not live in
temples built by human hands. And he is not served
by human hands, as if he needed anything. Rather, he
himself gives everyone life and breath and everything
else. From one man he made all the nations, that they
should inhabit the whole earth; and he marked out
their appointed times in history and the boundaries of
their lands. God did this so that they would seek him
and perhaps reach out for him and find him, though

he is not far from any one of us. "For in him we live and move and have our being." As some of your own poets have said, "We are his offspring."
ACTS 17:24-28, NIV

I used to think if my phone rang, I needed to answer it because if someone called me, then God must need me to help that person. Combine that with my other bondage of thinking I had to get everything right, and you can imagine how weary I became.

Do you know what being connected to my heart has taught me? It has taught me that if my phone rings and I can't get to it, or better yet, I don't *want* to get it or don't have time right then to get it, God is big enough to handle that. If the person calling really needs help, God can arrange for someone else to help him or her. The Lord of the universe is absolutely capable of that. It's not all up to us. And when we fall into thinking it is, we get into trouble because the enemy loves to use our best intentions to wear us out. (I told you this was a sneaky one.)

No, God really does not need us.

But—and this is important—God does desire to use us.

He wants us to join in this amazing, redeeming story that he is writing. He even has an important role in mind for each of us. It's just when I start thinking the play can't go on without me that I am entering into dangerous—and exhausting—territory.

Jesus told the Pharisees that if his disciples kept quiet instead of praising him, "the stones would immediately cry out" (Luke 19:40). The truth is that God can use anything for his purposes. In Exodus 3, he used a burning bush to communicate with Moses. In Numbers 22, he used a talking donkey to speak to a disobedient prophet named Balaam. But even in those cases, he used the bush and the donkey to get through to the heart of a human being.

That's what God is always after. He is after our hearts.

He is after our hearts to be after *his* heart.

"Seek first the kingdom of God and His righteousness," Jesus said in Matthew 6:33. And the way to God's Kingdom is Jesus himself. It is him we should be seeking—not our work, not our ministry, not our duties or those we think need us. Jesus first. And then, as we continue to seek him, to abide in him, he will lead us into the ministry he has in mind for us. He will give us strength in the middle of long seasons of battle or disappointment. He will give us the grace to overcome even the most ravaging of sins. And he will take care of the needs that we are so desperately striving to meet—perhaps through us or perhaps through someone else.

> Come to me, all you who are weary and burdened, and
> I will give you rest. Take my yoke upon you and learn
> from me, for I am gentle and humble in heart, and you
> will find rest for your souls. For my yoke is easy and
> my burden is light.
>
> MATTHEW 11:28-30, NIV

That is the life Jesus calls us to. The burden he has for us is easy and light, not wearisome. It is our pride, our distorted belief that God needs us in order to get anything important done, that has strapped these oppressive yokes on us. God gives rest, not exhaustion.

Am I saying that if we persist in seeking God's Kingdom, we will never feel tired? Of course not. We live in finite bodies that can only do so much, and we live in a fallen world that can drive us to the edges of our endurance. Even when we are seeking God first and following his lead instead of our own egos, there will be days or seasons that push us past our comfort zone.

Ask Elijah, who grew weary doing exactly what God was calling him to. Or Job, who, as we're clearly told, did nothing wrong or sinful and yet grew so weary he was ready to give up. Or Moses, who was weary from the mental roller coaster Pharaoh had put him on and the sheer physical exertion of holding up his arms. Or me after one of our VBS for women events!

You see, there's a big difference between the ordinary weariness of a tired body and brain and the sinful weariness of a shut-down heart. Whenever we weary ourselves out of a prideful need to "do it myself" or "do it all" or when we refuse God's offer of rest in our weariness, we risk developing a sinful, shut-down heart. As I see it, it's all a basic issue of staying clear on who needs whom.

Think of those first few moments after the fall of Adam and Eve, those moments when the revelation of their sin came down swift and hard. There was absolutely nothing they could do at that point. Never has there been a time when humanity was more in need of God. Adam and Eve—and all of us who have come after them—desperately needed a plan. And what needed to be done was something we couldn't accomplish.

But God could. He had a plan, prepared out of his infinite love before we ever sinned. That is our God. He goes before us. Before we get to the point of our own need, he has already provided for the need.

Do you remember the story in Genesis 22 about Abraham taking Isaac up to Mount Moriah to be sacrificed? God had a plan then too. Even as Abraham climbed that mountain—his heart anguished over what he feared he would have to do, his obedience weighing heavy on his heart—God was making provision for the sacrifice. I can just imagine God coming up the other side of the mountain with that ram for Abraham to sacrifice in Isaac's place.

We have needed God from the beginning of time. And we continue to need him today. He is the one in whom we still "live and move and have our being" (Acts 17:28). To deceive ourselves with the lie that God needs us instead of the other way around can project us into a painful place of pride that will ultimately wear us out.

Reclaiming the Weary Heart

As always, reclaiming the weary heart requires recognition. We must be willing to be honest with where we are and what has gotten us here—whether we are merely tired or are weary because we have believed the lie of the weary heart. As in the case of the fearful heart, we need to get curious about our motives—and whether we need to repent of pride that is driving us harder and further than God ever intended. And then we need to consider what God is really calling us to—whether he wants us to push on a little further, relying on his strength, or whether it's time to back off from what we've been doing and rest.

Don't underestimate the power of a little rest! Often all we really need is to take advantage of the respite that our God, who knows us better than anyone, wants to provide for us.

Think of the familiar words of the Twenty-third Psalm:

The Lord is my shepherd, I lack nothing.
    He *makes me* lie down in green pastures,
he *leads me* beside quiet waters,
    he refreshes my soul.
vv. 1-3, niv (emphasis added)

Whenever I read this passage of Scripture, I am struck by the nuance of the language. These verses speak of our need, God's understanding of our need, and his knowledge of how we resist our need. We do need to lie down in green pastures. We do need moments where we walk beside still waters. But sometimes, like children at bedtime, we fight against the rest we need so badly, so he has to *make* us do it. Other times he will be able to simply lead us gently toward what we need.

And what is the end result? A refreshing. A renewing. And something even more beautiful: a sweet encounter with the heart of our Father. I love the way the *Jewish Study Bible* translates this: "He leads me to water in places of repose; He renews my life."[2]

That's exactly what he offered Elijah at a time when he was running from the angry Queen Jezebel and weary to the point of exhaustion.

When Elijah saw how things were, he ran for dear life to Beersheba, far in the south of Judah. He left his young servant there and then went on into the desert another day's journey. He came to a lone broom bush and collapsed in its shade, wanting in the worst way to be done with it all—to just die: "Enough of this, GOD! Take my life—I'm ready to join my ancestors in the grave!" Exhausted, he fell asleep under the lone broom bush.

Suddenly an angel shook him awake and said, "Get up and eat!"

He looked around and, to his surprise, right by his head were a loaf of bread baked on some coals and a jug of water. He ate the meal and went back to sleep.

The angel of GOD came back, shook him awake again, and said, "Get up and eat some more—you've got a long journey ahead of you."

He got up, ate and drank his fill, and set out.
Nourished by that meal, he walked forty days and
nights, all the way to the mountain of God, to Horeb.
When he got there, he crawled into a cave and went to
sleep.

1 KINGS 19:3–9, *The Message*

Elijah was simply exhausted—mentally and physically and
probably spiritually as well. He desperately needed nourishment
and rest. And sometimes that is true of us, especially when we
have pushed ourselves too hard in the mistaken belief that God
needs us. As Joyce Meyer writes:

If you are feeling compelled to do so much that you
are physically worn out, you may be driven instead of
led. Remember, you have to come apart from a busy
routine before you come apart yourself. You have to get
away from everything before you come apart physically,
mentally, and emotionally. Give yourself time to get a
good night's sleep.

It is tempting to do everything that everybody else
is doing, be involved in everything, know everything,
hear everything, and be everywhere, but it isn't God's
best for you. Be willing to separate yourself from com-
pulsive activity before you come apart at the seams![3]

A while back, after completing a VBS for women event
here in Franklin, Philly and I loaded the car and headed to
South Carolina to start another VBS for women. We finished
the Franklin event on Tuesday and left for Carolina (by way of
Atlanta) on Wednesday to prepare for a Sunday night event.
To tell you I was weary would be a huge understatement. After

weeks of planning, then three long days with nightly teaching, ministering afterward, and very little sleep, I was beyond exhausted.

Poor Philly! He was the one who had to deal with me as I climbed into the car that Wednesday and proceeded to fall apart.

"I can't do this. This is too much. Ministry is too hard. I don't have anything left to give anyone. I was so stupid planning another one of these events right after the other. I just can't do it. Welcome to the ministry!" I added to my still-newlywed husband.

He was so gracious. He simply listened and let me cry as we drove to Atlanta and checked into a hotel, where he had some professional meetings the next day.

The following morning I think I woke up around eleven. I can't tell you the last time I have slept until eleven. I ordered a big, juicy hamburger, French fries, and a large Coke and had it sent to my room so I could eat in my pj's. Then I put on my bathing suit, grabbed a book that was purely for pleasure reading, and went out to sit by the pool. I swam. I read. I talked to my cousin on the phone and caught up with normal life. And with each passing moment, my heart felt more alive. More refreshed. Less weary.

The next morning I did the same thing. And by the time we pulled out later that afternoon, I was ready for the upcoming VBS. More than that, I was excited. All I had needed in those moments was some physical and mental rest.

That to me is the beauty of God's gift of the Sabbath. When God rested on the seventh day and wrote a Sabbath into our story, it wasn't because he was weary. God doesn't get weary. He doesn't need rest. He was modeling for us what we, with our human flesh, need so we can function at our best and fulfill our part in what he wants to do.

In Mark 2, Jesus told us clearly what the Sabbath is all about: "The Sabbath day was made for man. Man was not made for the Sabbath day" (v. 27, NIrv). He said that to the Pharisees, who had forgotten God's original purpose and turned the Sabbath into another set of rules to keep instead of the restful gift God intended it to be.

Unfortunately the Pharisaic mentality has persisted over the centuries, with plenty of rules about what can happen on the Sabbath and what is forbidden. A few generations ago, any kind of work was frowned on, even cooking. Reading any book but the Bible was frowned on. And movies—God forbid!

But those kinds of rules completely missed what Jesus was saying about the purpose of the Sabbath. As Matthew Henry explains it, "The sabbath is a sacred and divine institution; but we must receive and embrace it as a privilege and a benefit, not as a task and a drudgery."[4]

I have come to see the Sabbath as a gift of time. Time to take our kids to church and worship together as a family. Time to have Sunday dinner with my family around the table. (They call it lunch; I call it dinner. If I called it lunch, they might think I was going to cook again later.) I cook fried chicken and rice and gravy and homemade biscuits. We talk and laugh and linger around the table. (Well, some of us do. Others ask to be excused and go off to play, and that is okay too.) I have come to look forward to Sunday afternoon naps and an early evening Coca-Cola.

When we have the kids, we'll often play a game in the evening. If it is just Philly and me, he may watch football while I read or we may catch up on one of our favorite shows or go play a round of golf. We recuperate and rejuvenate so we will have something to offer the week ahead. It is such a sweet time for us. And I have come to see it as vital to my ministry.

I love what Senator Joe Lieberman says in his book *The Gift of Rest*, which he wrote to explain his observance of the Jewish Sabbath. People often ask this four-term senator from Connecticut, "How can you stop all your work as a senator to observe the Sabbath each week?" And Lieberman answers, "How could I do all my work as a senator if I did *not* stop to observe the Sabbath each week?"[5]

The world will not fall apart if we don't update our Facebook account or tweet our latest happenings or if we don't meet for another coffee or another lunch or we wait a day to answer an e-mail. But our world might well fall apart if we don't take time to rest. We need to allow our hearts to assume freedom, and that means freedom for our bodies and minds as well.

The Whisper of His Presence

Rest is essential to reclaiming a weary heart, but rest alone won't do it. We also need to spend time alone with God. This is what Elijah did after the angel provided him with nourishment.

> He got up, ate and drank his fill, and set out. Nourished by that meal, he walked forty days and nights, all the way to the mountain of God, to Horeb. When he got there, he crawled into a cave and went to sleep.
>
> Then the word of GOD came to him: "So Elijah, what are you doing here?"
>
> "I've been working my heart out for the GOD-of-the-Angel-Armies," said Elijah. "The people of Israel have abandoned your covenant, destroyed the places of worship, and murdered your prophets. I'm the only one left, and now they're trying to kill me."
>
> Then he was told, "Go, stand on the mountain at attention before GOD. GOD will pass by."

A hurricane wind ripped through the mountains
and shattered the rocks before GOD, but GOD wasn't
to be found in the wind; after the wind an earthquake,
but GOD wasn't in the earthquake; and after the
earthquake fire, but GOD wasn't in the fire; and after
the fire a gentle and quiet whisper.

I KINGS 19:8-12, *The Message*

How do we hear the whisper of God's presence? We have to
get quiet enough to hear him, and that usually means pulling
away from our everyday lives and spending time alone in his
presence.

God knew that Elijah needed to encounter him. He knows
we need this too. But weariness (and Satan's lies) can cause us
to feel that time with God is just another thing on the to-do
list, maybe even less important than our other to-dos. But it is
actually the one activity we cannot live without. If we take time
to encounter God, he will make himself known.

Time with God was vital to me in my time of weariness.
That day in Panera I had such a long list—my book deadlines,
preparing a lesson to teach, plus all those other tasks of running my home and my life. But what I needed most was God. I
needed his Word. And when I took the time to listen, he spoke
so sweetly to me. My time with him not only replenished me;
it also confirmed the words Deneen had spoken to me earlier
and helped me see what I needed to do.

Relationships Make a Difference

That brings us to the third vital element in reclaiming the weary
heart: relationships. It really helps to have people in our lives
who know all of our story, who can lovingly assess where we
really are and support us in our weariness.

When Moses stood on a hill, watching his people battle the Amalekites and holding up his hands, his arms grew tired and numb. This was a problem because the battle would only go in the Israelites' favor as long as he held up his arms. But Moses had help in his weariness:

> But Moses' hands were heavy and grew weary. So [the other men] took a stone and put it under him and he sat on it. Then Aaron and Hur held up his hands, one on one side and one on the other side; so his hands were steady until the going down of the sun.
> EXODUS 17:12, AMP

I have been blessed with so many people who offered me that kind of loving support when I needed it so desperately. I honestly don't think I would have survived my divorce if not for God's wonderful gift of my family and of friends like Deneen, people whose prayers and practical support kept me going when I couldn't take another step. Since I've known Philly, he too has been a precious source of support in my life—a speaker of encouraging words and difficult truths I need to hear and a really good listener. (I hope I am a source of loving support to him as well.)

The beauty of these supportive relationships is that they don't just move in to prop me up when I'm tired. These special people in my life are also willing to be honest with me. That's what Deneen did for me that day in Panera. She spoke truth into my weariness much as Moses' father-in-law spoke truth into his life:

> The next day Moses took his place to judge the people. People were standing before him all day long, from morning to night. When Moses' father-in-law saw all that he was doing for the people, he said, "What's

going on here? Why are you doing all this, and all by yourself, letting everybody line up before you from morning to night?"

Moses said to his father-in-law, "Because the people come to me with questions about God. When something comes up, they come to me. I judge between a man and his neighbor and teach them God's laws and instructions."

Moses' father-in-law said, "This is no way to go about it. You'll burn out, and the people right along with you. This is way too much for you—you can't do this alone. Now listen to me. Let me tell you how to do this so that God will be in this with you. Be there for the people before God, but let the matters of concern be presented to God. Your job is to teach them the rules and instructions, to show them how to live, what to do. And then you need to keep a sharp eye out for competent men—men who fear God, men of integrity, men who are incorruptible—and appoint them as leaders over groups organized by the thousand, by the hundred, by fifty, and by ten. They'll be responsible for the everyday work of judging among the people. They'll bring the hard cases to you, but in the routine cases they'll be the judges. They will share your load and that will make it easier for you. If you handle the work this way, you'll have the strength to carry out whatever God commands you, and the people in their settings will flourish also."

EXODUS 18:13-23, *The Message*

What a gift this was to Moses. His father-in-law looked at all that Moses was doing and told him it was too much. It was a gift to me as well, because this was the passage I was reading in Panera, the one that confirmed Deneen's honest and loving advice. I am so grateful for friends who are willing to speak that kind of truth to me.

Those are the kinds of relationships toward which alive hearts gravitate. And those are the types of relationships that keep hearts alive.

Time for a Change

Moses' father-in-law told him in no uncertain terms that if he kept up his pace, he was going to wear out, and the people he was leading would suffer as well. This is true for many of us who have taken on too much and have begun to shut down in weariness. In an attempt to seem perfect, in an inability to say no, in a distorted thought that God needs us to do what we're doing, many of us have taken on tasks that God has not asked us to do, tasks we don't need to be doing. And if we keep doing them, everyone will suffer.

That is what I learned in my time of profound weariness. I didn't want to let go of the commitment I'd discussed with Deneen—a commitment that allowed me to spend more time with my kids. I felt that if God put me in the lives of these children, he must need me to be physically present for every moment they are with us. But that mind-set had made me so weary that not only was I miserable, but my influence on our kids was lessened as well.

Ken Edwards once said something to Philly and me that had a powerful impact on both of us. Like many blended families, we struggled with the amount of time our kids would be with us, and we had some inevitable sadness about the limits on our time with them. But one day when we were complaining about this, Ken told us, "The scope of where you can operate might be diminished, but your impact won't be."

As I sat there in Panera, I realized that Ken's advice applied to my weariness as well. If I stubbornly refused to narrow my scope, my impact would suffer. So I had to make some changes.

That brings us to the final step we may need to take in reclaiming a weary heart. Once we have recognized our weary heart, repented of it, and gotten some rest, some changes may be in order.

For some of us, like me, change may mean letting go of something, backing off from an activity, an involvement, a ministry, even a relationship. It probably won't be easy to do that. Backing off may feel foolish, weak, even selfish, but it isn't—not as long as we make the decision carefully and prayerfully. There will be seasons when we carry the big things and seasons when God will want our loads lightened, and we need to be okay with whatever he is asking.

For others of us, making a change may mean we need to quit avoiding God. Often people ensnared in sin will tell themselves they're trying to clean themselves up *before* they come to him. But they're usually just fooling themselves.

The idea of trying to fight sin until we're bloody communicates clearly an illusion of self-sufficiency. We are not self-sufficient. We are people in desperate need of a holy and able Father. God doesn't need us to master our sin before we come to him. God needs us to own our sin and surrender it, all of it, so he can relieve us of the wearying weight of it.

Renewing Our Strength

My friend, we don't have to do it all. We were never intended to. Yes, we are called by our loving Creator. But this is what we were called to:

Have you not known? Have you not heard? The
everlasting God, the Lord, the Creator of the ends of
the earth, does not faint or grow weary; there is no
searching of His understanding.

He gives power to the faint and weary, and to him
who has no might He increases strength [causing it to
multiply and making it to abound].

Even youths shall faint and be weary, and [selected]
young men shall feebly stumble and fall exhausted;

But those who wait for the Lord [who expect, look
for, and hope in Him] shall change and renew their
strength and power; they shall lift their wings and
mount up [close to God] as eagles [mount up to the
sun]; they shall run and not be weary, they shall walk
and not faint or become tired.

ISAIAH 40:28-31, AMP

What a beautiful expression of how God wants to work in our
weariness. But it can't happen when we shut down our hearts in
pride and stubbornness. When we expect God to work and relax
our expectations of doing it all, when we depend on him and realize he is not depending on us, when we put our hope in God and
realize that, as much as he loves us, he doesn't require our help to
accomplish his purposes—that is when our strength is renewed.
It happens when we are waiting on him and depending on him
and when we keep clear about who needs whom.

I'm finally getting it through my head that I can't meet with
everyone who wants to do lunch or come to me for counseling. I can't answer all the e-mails on the same day they arrive or
produce one book after another without time off in between.
And I am learning to walk in the freedom of that truth and take
advantage of God's gift of refreshment.

I'm learning, for instance, to ask honestly for the time I need instead of promising and then killing myself to deliver. I am also learning to set aside alone time without apologizing. I need time alone not only because of what I do but because quiet and aloneness are places of refreshment to me. And gradually, steadily, I am learning to let go of what God doesn't need me to do. This new season in my life has again revealed more tasks I need to release in order to be truly present for the deep moments of real impact.

That weary day in Panera, I really thought I was having a breakdown.

My sweet husband said later, "No, babe, I think you've had a breakthrough."

And you know what? He was right.

That difficult episode forced me to come to the end of my prideful self. It forced me to recognize that I'd believed the lie of the weary heart—to recognize that God desires me, loves me, uses me, but he doesn't need me. All he really expects from me is to stay close to him, ask what he wants from me, then take up his light and easy yoke.

And I can relax—because he will do the rest.

CHAPTER TWELVE

LIVING WITH A RECLAIMED HEART

*Listen to your life. See it for the fathomless mystery that
it is. In the boredom and pain of it no less than in the
excitement and gladness: touch, taste, smell your way to
the holy and hidden heart of it because in the last analysis
all moments are key moments, and life itself is grace.*

FREDERICK BUECHNER

IN CASE you haven't figured it out by now, I'm a Southern girl.
I also love movies and fried food. So it probably won't surprise
you that the very Southern movie *Fried Green Tomatoes* is a
favorite of mine. One reason I love it is that the main character,
Evelyn Couch (played by Kathy Bates), goes on a journey to
reclaim her heart. For most of her forty years, Evelyn has been
swallowed whole by fear, which has manifested itself through
overeating, extreme people pleasing, and other forms of hiding.
She has forgotten how to live—that is, until she visits a nursing
home and meets a feisty resident named Ninny (Jessica Tandy).
Ninny tells her stories about the adventures of two young
women who ran a café in the little railroad town of Whistle
Stop, Alabama. Ninny also confesses to Evelyn that she has an
alter ego named Towanda, who steps in when she needs to do

something brave or take charge of her life. Over time, Evelyn develops an odd but beautiful friendship with Ninny. And as she does, Evelyn also begins to reclaim her heart.

One of the most defining scenes happens in the parking lot of a grocery store. Sweet, timid Evelyn is in her car, waiting for another customer to pull out of a space. But just as the other car pulls out, Evelyn is cut off by two young girls with really bad perms (gotta love the eighties!). Their fire-engine-red VW convertible whips into the space Evelyn has been patiently waiting for. She tells them nicely that she had been waiting for that parking spot. They snap back with a mean-spirited comment and head for the store, leaving Evelyn to stare at the bumper of the car that has taken her space.

What follows is powerful, though ill-advised, and absolutely hilarious. You see the change as it sweeps over Evelyn's face, her decision to do life differently. Her look of dejection slowly turns into one of determination. She whispers, "Towanda," as she stomps on the accelerator and rams her car smack-dab into the VW's rear end. Then she backs up and does it all over again— about five times!

Now I am not suggesting you play bumper cars in the Kroger parking lot in order to reclaim your heart. But sometimes extreme visuals like this reiterate what it means to live alive. To no longer let our hearts be violated, manipulated, abused, or lied to.

My prayer for you is that as you've read the pages of this book, you have had your own Towanda moments of recognition and decision. Recognition that clearly revealed to you what you've allowed the enemy to steal from you with his lies. And a decision that, with God's help, you will never let that happen again.

But as we have said so many times, this is a journey and not a destination.

Will some change happen quickly? Possibly. My shame fell off me in one moment of my Father speaking to my heart about how he saw me. I once watched a young woman weep uncontrollably as God instantaneously broke off one of the enemy's lies to her heart. It was powerful and real, and it happened suddenly.

But moments like that are rare. It's far more likely that reclaiming a shut-down heart will happen slowly and gradually. Day by day, moment by moment, you'll have to decide whether you will revert to your old shut-down patterns of behavior or fight for your freedom to live as God designed you. And shutting down will always be a temptation because while reclaiming your heart brings joy and freedom, it also puts you at risk for pain.

I experienced this in the early months of my marriage to Philly. The pain I experienced in dealing with one of our children (who of course was hurting too) was so deep and excruciating that I just wanted to run away and hide. Actually, as I've already mentioned, I *did* hide a lot—in my closet. And it was in that closet that the Lord gave me a gentle but stern reminder. He reminded me of all the years I had lived shut down and how hard I had worked and all the pain I had been through to get my heart back. I could choose to shut down again. But if I did that, I would thwart all he had planned for me on this adventure with my children.

The sad truth is, shutting down our hearts is always a possibility at any time of our lives. Sometimes it feels like the only safe choice because, as C. S. Lewis so memorably wrote:

> To love at all is to be vulnerable. Love anything, and
> your heart will certainly be wrung and possibly be
> broken. If you want to make sure of keeping it intact,

you must give your heart to no one, not even to an animal. Wrap it carefully round with hobbies and little luxuries; avoid all entanglements; lock it up safe in the casket or coffin of your selfishness. But in that casket—safe, dark, motionless, airless—it will change. It will not be broken; it will become unbreakable, impenetrable, irredeemable. The alternative to tragedy, or at least to the risk of tragedy, is damnation. The only place outside Heaven where you can be perfectly safe from all the dangers and perturbations of love is Hell.[1]

Seek Out the Word

The most important thing you can do on the journey to reclaim your heart is to stay grounded in the Word of God. It's your dependable source of truth to counter the enemy's lies. I urge you to seek out its wisdom and guidance as if you were mining for gold—because that's exactly what you will be doing. Nothing is more valuable, more precious to living free and alive than the words of Scripture.

Hebrews 4:12 assures us that "the word of God is alive and active. Sharper than any double-edged sword, it penetrates even to dividing soul and spirit, joints and marrow; it judges the thoughts and attitudes of the heart" (NIV). This is why the enemy tries so hard to keep us from the Bible—because it's a living and powerful thing. With the precision of a surgeon, it can reach into the deepest places of our hearts, extracting Satan's lies and revealing God's truth. The more we read it, study it, and reflect on it, the more it becomes a part of us. And the more it's a part of us, the better able we are to see ourselves rightly and resist the lies of the enemy.

Remember, the common denominator of shut-down hearts is that they're based on a lie. Falsehood is fundamental to the enemy's nature; he doesn't know how to be any other way. John 8:44 defines him as "the father of lies and of all that is false" (AMP).

On top of that, Jeremiah 17:9 reminds us that we cannot even always trust our own hearts and minds because "the heart is deceitful above all things. . . . Who can know it?" Like Adam and Eve, we are easily swayed not only by the enemy's lies, but also by our own sin and selfishness. We are prone to fooling ourselves and letting ourselves be fooled.

How do we combat the enemy's lies and our own foolishness? With the truth. But to do that, we have to *know* the truth. In fact, we need to be reminded of the truth over and over. And the only way to do that is to stay close to the original Source. As Jesus told his followers, "If you abide in My word [hold fast to My teachings and live in accordance with them], you are truly My disciples. And you will know the Truth, and the Truth will set you free" (John 8:31-32, AMP).

Jesus himself used the Word of God against the enemy. The most obvious instance of this is the story of Jesus' temptation in the wilderness (Luke 4:1-13). Again and again, Satan came to Jesus with twisted half-truths, trying to persuade him to abandon his mission, and in each encounter Jesus challenged Satan with words of Scripture. He came at Jesus here the same way he came at Eve, appealing to the lust of the eyes, the lust of the flesh, and the pride of life. And he failed utterly. As Jesus spoke truth by declaring the Word of God, eventually the lies were broken. Satan was defeated, and then he left. It is no different for us today. We thwart Satan's schemes by knowing and speaking scriptural truth.

In that season of my life when I was so broken, I found I had to dig into the Word for my very survival. It was the only way I didn't completely crumble underneath the lies the enemy was trying to consume me with. I had to trust and believe that

- if I didn't throw away my confidence, it would be richly rewarded and I would receive all that God had promised (Hebrews 10:35-36, NIV).
- I would see the goodness of the Lord in the land of the living (Psalm 27:13).
- God would perfect all that concerned me (Psalm 138:8).
- goodness and mercy would follow me all the days of my life (Psalm 23:6).
- he who had begun a good work in me would carry it on to completion (Philippians 1:6, NIV).
- if I built my house upon the rock, it would not fall when the rains came and the floods rose (Matthew 7:24-25).
- if I kept my heart pure, I would see God (Matthew 5:8).

Those truths and thousands of others like them were what kept me sane. They were what kept my heart alive when the enemy of my soul was determined to shut it down.

Ask Questions

Another practice for the journey of reclaiming our hearts is learning to ask God questions about our heart issues. The Bible invites us to do this and promises that God wants to answer when we ask:

> Don't bargain with God. Be direct. Ask for what you need. This isn't a cat-and-mouse, hide-and-seek game we're in. If your child asks for bread, do you trick him with sawdust? If he asks for fish, do you scare him with a live snake on his plate? As bad as you are, you wouldn't think of such a thing. You're at least decent to your own children. So don't you think the God who conceived you in love will be even better?
>
> MATTHEW 7:7-11, *The Message*

But asking questions isn't necessarily a matter of unloading a list of queries during prayer time. Sometimes it's more a matter of paying attention to what is going on around and within us. When we observe something that feels out of place, we need to ask God about it with an open mind, then wait expectantly for an answer. When I do this, I'm often surprised by the insights I receive.

One night, while we were at the dinner table, our middle child walked over to the sink and wrapped a rubber band around the spray nozzle. She did it in such a way that whoever turned the water on would immediately be sprayed. Then she looked at her dad and said, "Hey, Dad, come turn the water on." (She's still learning that successful pranks aren't usually announced.) But her dad never did it because in the meantime our little one had a roaring meltdown. I don't even remember what it was about. I just know it was loud and extreme—and distracting.

A few minutes later, in the middle of all that chaos, I got up to rinse off my dinner plate, forgetting about the rubber band on the spray nozzle. So when I turned the water on, which I have a tendency to do to its full capacity, I got drenched from my neck to my waist.

The entire table looked at me in shock. Even the child going through a breakdown stopped and stared.

That was when my husband snickered.

Every ounce of blood rushed to my face and my head at that moment. I even felt my anger in the pulse in my temples. I looked at the prankster child and asked her, as calmly as I could manage, not to do that rubber-band trick again. I turned to Philly and said, "You can do the dishes." Then I fled the kitchen. But as I headed to my closet, my sanctuary of choice, I heard everyone at the table laughing, including the child who only moments before had been having the ultimate conniption.

I walked straight to the closet, sat on the floor, and sobbed. And here's the thing—I knew it was ridiculous to get so upset over something like that. My head knew that full well. But my heart—wow, my heart couldn't reconcile that at all.

A little while later Philly came to find me, and he was still laughing. You can only imagine how well that went over. I was still angry—especially because I didn't understand *why* I was so angry.

A few weeks afterward, when we were at my parents' house around the dinner table, I shared this story with them and some of my closest friends. And of course, what did they do? They laughed. Why not? It's funny . . . now.

But as they were laughing, I asked out loud, "I wonder why pranks like that make me so angry." As soon as I asked the question, a possible answer came straight into my heart: "Maybe it's because they make me feel devalued."

Asking my heart that question helped me understand why that one simple action had taken me to such a broken place. My precious daughter wasn't trying to devalue me that day. She was simply trying to enjoy her father. Yet, because of the broken places of my own heart, I was unable to be a part of that. My "How dare you!" sirens started wailing, and it was downhill from there.

Whenever we experience something like I did—this huge emotional reaction to some small offense—it's a good sign that something's going on inside us. And when that happens, the sweetest gift we can offer our hearts is to ask God what it is. Asking leads to recognition, which can then allow us to repent and take the necessary steps to change our behavior.

As I've mentioned before, Philly and I often discern heart issues by looking for patterns of behavior. When things form a pattern, we can usually see that there might be something we need to ask questions about. Avoidance—leaving the mail in the mailbox, not answering the phone—can be a pattern. Perpetual distractions—hours in front of the TV or with video games or incessant shopping—can be a pattern. Manipulative behavior—whining or telling little white lies to avoid the truth—can be a pattern. Any kind of behavior becomes a pattern if it's repeated under certain circumstances. And patterns are clear indicators of something we need to pay attention to. But if we are unwilling to ask God questions because we are too afraid of the answer we may receive, then we will never get to the other side of the pain. And we will find ourselves climbing right back into our prison cell.

Stay Vigilant

Remember the Proverbs verse from the beginning of our study: "Above all else, guard your heart"? Look at this verse in context and in a different translation:

> Dear friend, listen well to my words;
>   tune your ears to my voice.
> Keep my message in plain view at all times.
>   Concentrate! Learn it by heart!
> Those who discover these words live, really live;
>   body and soul, they're bursting with health.
>
> *Keep vigilant watch over your heart;*
>   that's *where life starts.*
> Don't talk out of both sides of your mouth;
>   avoid careless banter, white lies, and gossip.
> Keep your eyes straight ahead;
>   ignore all *sideshow distractions.*
> Watch your step,

and the road will stretch out smooth before you.
Look neither right nor left;
    leave evil in the dust.

PROVERBS 4:20-27, *The Message* (EMPHASIS ADDED)

What comes to mind when you hear the word *vigilant?* That is a war word to me. A William Wallace word. A Maximus word. Or if you have never seen *Braveheart* or *Gladiator*, think of it as a Towanda word. It's a declaration of war in the battle for our hearts, a refusal to surrender or give in.

That is why God says we are to be *vigilant!* It is a war word for a reason—because we are in a battle. Our enemy is relentless, and he has multiple weapons of attack. If he can't get us one way, he will come at us another way. When we've recognized him in one area, he will show up in an area we never dreamed. And this will not end until Eden is restored and Jesus comes back. Therefore, we are to be watching over our hearts at all times.

"It feels easier to stay where I am."

I have no doubt.

"This seems like too much work."

More work than you can even imagine.

"If I keep my heart open and alive, I will just set myself up to be hurt again."

You can count on it.

What you are willing to do with your own heart is up to you. But I really, really hope you'll choose to be vigilant because the alternative is heartbreaking. And I mean that literally.

Don't Get Distracted

Now look back at that Proverbs passage to see what gets in the way of this vigilance. "Sideshow distractions." They come in all shapes and sizes. The enemy loves distractions and is always throwing them our way.

In fact, these feelings and behaviors that shut down our hearts are essentially distractions. Anger is a distraction. Shame is a distraction. Performance is a distraction. Fear is a distraction. These are all simply places we choose to hide out, ways of avoiding our real heart issues. But they are by no means the only distractions we might choose. Almost anything in life—work, hobbies, relationships, addictions—can be used to hide from pain and keep us from living our real lives.

You may have wondered why there hasn't been a chapter on the addicted heart. Honestly, I thought there would be. But I realized as I worked through these chapters that most addictions are essentially symptoms of far deeper issues. Heart issues. I'm aware there may be other issues as well, so I don't want to make this sound overly simplistic. But I am convinced the reason so many recovering addicts return to their addictive behaviors is that the underlying heart issues haven't been addressed. Whether we're talking about alcohol, drugs, sex, food, entertainment, or work, addictions are usually ways to escape from pain or discomfort. They too are essentially distractions.

Stay Present

Reclaiming our hearts and keeping them open is not just a matter of vigilantly avoiding distraction, however. In fact, it's pretty easy to deduce that the more emphasis we place on the distraction, the more it remains in the forefront and the more we are distracted by it. So it's even more essential to keep the value of our hearts front and center. This is an intentional process. And one of the best ways to do it is by staying present in our lives.

When Ken Edwards came and spoke to our "Reclaiming Your Heart" study, someone asked him, "Where do I even *start?*"

He said something many of those in the room that day may not have understood. "Start with tasting your food."

I knew exactly what he was talking about. Many of us are so task driven that even eating becomes a "to do." But God gave us life to be *lived*.

I love to watch one of my closest friends eat. She savors every bite. That first bite she puts in her mouth goes in so slowly, and then you watch as the recognition of how good it is crosses her face. Recently I was with her in Charleston, South Carolina, and she introduced me to one of my new favorite restaurants, Halls Chophouse on King Street. We went to their Sunday brunch. She ordered an omelet and cheese grits with a side of collards, and I ordered the sausage gravy and biscuits.

This was shortly after Ken had spoken to my study about tasting our food, so I paid extra-close attention to my friend this day. And as I watched her, I smiled. That woman takes every morsel of life in and experiences it. She is about to turn fifty, and yet just a few years ago she was my cohort at Disneyland when we tried to beat out a group of teenagers to be first in line on Space Mountain.

Friends, when is the last time you tasted your food? I mean, truly tasted it? And when is the last time you have been fully present to all that is going on in your life?

Being present in this beautiful life God has given us to enjoy provides a far easier path to staying connected to him and his truth than focusing on avoiding the things that would distract us.

This is what GOD says,
>the God who builds a road right through the ocean,
>who carves a path through pounding waves,
The God who summons horses and chariots and armies—
>they lie down and then can't get up;

they're snuffed out like so many candles:
"Forget about what's happened;
    don't keep going over old history.
Be alert, be present. I'm about to do something
        brand-new.
    It's bursting out! Don't you see it?"
ISAIAH 43:16-19, *The Message*

God wants to do something new for us. But he can't do something new when we are living in a land of distractions. Distractions keep us looking backward at the things that hold us captive. Being present has us keeping our eyes on him. On what he has given us to enjoy. On the beauty that surrounds us. And it is only in being present that we can enjoy the new things he has to offer.

What Makes You Come Alive?

It's not enough just to avoid distractions and be present for whatever life throws at you. It's also vital to rediscover what makes you come alive—and *do* it as much as you can.

In chapter 1 we looked at John 10:10: "I have come that they may have life, and have it to the full" (NIV)—or, in the KJV, "more abundantly." *The Message* adds another layer to that meaning: "I came so they can have real and eternal life, more and better life than they ever dreamed of."

When is the last time you did something that left you breathless? That truly excited you? That refreshed you and rested you or just made you feel joyful?

Not long ago I talked with a young man who is on a vigilant quest to reclaim his heart. He said, "I don't even remember what I enjoy." It's easy to get to that point, isn't it? To get so involved in doing life that we miss actually living.

Many of the men I know do it by becoming consumed with work, their need to produce, the demands on their manhood. Women do it too, with their own jobs or families. We even do it in our churches, focusing on all the things we're supposed to do for God. The very idea of doing something just for us might make us feel a little guilty, like we're somehow cheating or doing the wrong thing. But I've come to believe that we're cheating on our very lives if we neglect to seek out those activities and pursuits that refresh and enliven us.

That's what golf was for me.

My first year of bonus-momdom absolutely consumed me. I had wanted all my life to be a mom, and I was absolutely determined not to waste a moment of it. But I got so involved in cooking and cleaning and couponing and carpooling and comforting broken hearts when our children were with us—as well as keeping up my work of writing and teaching—that I forgot I existed in all of that.

And then came the golf lessons. It wasn't about being a wife or mom. It wasn't about writing books or teaching Bible studies. It was something I did just for me. And I absolutely fell in love with it. The beauty of the landscape. The satisfaction of a good swing. The rhythms that were so different from my daily life. For me, at least, the time out there with my husband has been a wonderful plus. I honestly think that my days on the golf course refresh me so that I'm a better bonus mom, a better writer and teacher. I bring that sense of being more alive into all my other pursuits.

Now please understand. I'm not saying that our jobs can't bring us joy and help us feel alive. There is probably no place I feel more alive than when I am teaching. Nor am I saying that doing things for other people is at odds with living the abundant life we're called to. When my husband and kids enjoy a meal I've cooked, I find exceptional joy in that. And I'm certainly not saying we need to leave church or go on a permanent vacation in order to live abundantly—though I have to admit there are times when the idea is very appealing.

I'm saying that *all* of life has been created for our enjoyment as well as for our character development. Rapids are there to raft down. Waves are for people to surf on and bob in. Mountains are to be climbed. Children are to be delighted in.

Paul wrote in the book of Romans, "He who did not withhold or spare [even] His own Son but gave Him up for us all, will He not also with Him freely and graciously give us all [other] things?" (8:32, AMP). God's gift of life began with creation and was fulfilled in Christ. That's all we need, of course—but then he gives us more! The abundant life includes so many additional gifts for us to enjoy, to help us comprehend his love and care. I am absolutely convinced that I honor him when I enjoy a good book or a walk on the beach and celebrate his gift of life.

So what makes you come alive? It's time to give yourself permission to remember that—or rediscover it or discover it for the first time. Maybe joining the gym will do it—or taking golf lessons or signing up for a cooking class or dusting off the piano bench. Maybe you need a vacation or a night out without the kids or a long, leisurely bath. Then again, it might mean seeking another job or visiting a new church. The point is to make living fully—not just getting by—a priority and seek out ways to do that.

Look for God in the Details

Finally we need to be people who look for God in their details.

Interestingly enough, it was this piece that made Philly the most skeptical of me when we first met. I pretty much see God in everything, and I thank him for anything good that happens in my life. I don't know how *not* to do that. I believe it is the truth of James 1:16-18:

> Don't be deceived, my dear brothers and sisters. Every good and perfect gift is from above, coming down from the Father of the heavenly lights, who does not change like shifting shadows. He chose to give us birth through the word of truth, that we might be a kind of firstfruits of all he created (NIV).

Philly had lived a lot of years being manipulated by "Christianese"—the jargon that Christians fall into so easily. So when he encountered my tendency to see God in everything, he questioned its authenticity.

For instance, I would get my first taste of a McDonald's Coke on a Saturday morning and say, "Wow, God knows exactly what makes me happy."

Philly would say, "Well, what did you expect? If you go to McDonald's, you can be pretty certain that they are going to have Coke. It's just what McDonald's does. How is this God loving you in your details?"

But Philly's coming around—especially as he has witnessed what happens when we look for God's hand in our lives. I can now count quite a few times when he has picked up the phone and called me to share something that happened to him. Then come those words: "Babe, I really think God was loving me in my details." I will never get tired of hearing that. We've both learned that the more we look, expecting God to show up for us, the more evidence we find of his faithfulness even in little things.

What happened with my shih tzu Maggie is just one example.

I've always felt that, to comfort me in the pain of not having children, God has handpicked my dogs through the years. One of them was my sweet but ornery Maggie. She was a Valentine's gift from my first husband the first year we were married. I always called her Miss Independent. Maggie pretty much did things her way, ignoring most of my orders and carrying herself with an I'll-let-you-know-if-I-need-you air. It was so rare for her to come when she was called that when she lost her hearing as an old dog, it took me six months to realize it.

Still, Maggie was my buddy, and she was my constant companion through the painful years of my first marriage and then my divorce. I always said we would go together in the Rapture. But Maggie was getting older, and the Rapture didn't seem to be getting any closer. So I asked God to let her live at least until he had a new family for me.

It was a simple prayer, almost a child's prayer. I couldn't imagine life without my Maggie—especially being *alone* without her. God had already answered specific prayers for my other dog, Chloe, who had suffered with seizures for years. The seizures grew much worse, and it was clear she was suffering, but I couldn't bring myself to have her put down. So I asked the Lord to please take her in her sleep. He did. She died peacefully, just as I had prayed, a few months prior to my divorce.

God's act of kindness had revealed to my heart once again that he cared about my needs and my desires. So I trusted him to answer my prayer about Maggie.

A couple months after I met Philly, he said, "Maggie isn't quite herself tonight."

I said, "I know. She isn't."

But Maggie stayed with me as Philly and I spent time getting to know each other and realized we were in love. We got engaged and started preparing for our wedding, working our way through all the negotiations necessary to arrange a second marriage where kids were involved. Finally, on a day neither of us will ever forget, we married. And two weeks later, the weekend of the 2010 Tennessee floods, my Maggie died.

What a bittersweet day that was. I mourned my dog deeply. Poor Philly wasn't quite sure what to do with me. But even in the midst of my grief, I was acutely aware—and grateful—that God had answered my simple prayer about a dog.

My Maggie story is just one of hundreds of examples of the way God has expressed love to me in the details of my life. I could tell you story after story like that. You might think I'm a little crazy, but I'm okay with that. Quite honestly, I would rather spend my life looking for him and acknowledging him in my details than spend my life being skeptical and missing all the amazing ways he loves us, all the good and perfect gifts he bestows on us.

And the Journey Continues

As I look back over the last years and see the very personal, detailed way God has shown love to me, I am amazed. When I see what he has restored to me after a time of great loss, I am astounded. I'm not the same person I was a few years ago. My closest friends will attest to that. I am a woman who has found her heart and is working vigilantly to fight for it every day.

Recently Philly and I were talking about ways we used to respond and do things. We remind each other often of how shut down we were and how different we were before. And then we share our gratitude that even with all our still-broken parts, we are experiencing something that is real and beautiful.

We are present in our pain. And yes, there have been days that hurt us in our deepest places. There have been moments over the last few years when I've thought, *I didn't think I would ever hurt like this again.* But you know what? I'm glad I can feel that hurt because feeling it means I feel joy just as deeply.

When Philly played Pebble Beach, we experienced every ounce of beauty that day held. When I ate those fabulous biscuits and gravy at Halls Chophouse and sampled my friend's sweet-and-sour collards, I tasted every bit of them. When we rode our bikes on vacation last summer with our children, I watched in amazement at all of the painfully beautiful ways our hearts had collided that year. And I held on to my heart.

My friends, I don't have much to offer in this life. A GPA that barely got me out of college. A talent competition win and a top-ten finish in the Miss South Carolina pageant when bad perms reigned. A few novels about crazy Southern people.

But what I do have to offer is a heart that knows what it was like to be dead but has been granted the sweet privilege of coming back to life. I offer that to you.

As we wrap up this part of our journey together, please remember it is just that . . . a journey. Day by day, minute by minute, we all face the choice to die or live, to believe a lie or follow the truth, to shut down or open up, to do things our own way or abandon our hearts totally and completely to the heart of our Father. I hope you'll choose to protect your heart at all costs.

As you continue on this amazing journey, I hope you find yourself dreaming more often, loving more deeply, laughing more loudly, and living alive. Completely and totally alive.

The way your heart was always meant to be.

Notes

CHAPTER 1: HEART CHECK
1. John Eldredge, *Waking the Dead* (Nashville: Thomas Nelson, 2003), 9.

CHAPTER 2: GOT HEART?
1. To get a sense of some of these different perspectives, you can check out these resources: Trent C. Butler, ed., *Holman Bible Dictionary*, 1991, s.v. "heart," http://www.studylight.org/dic/hbd/view.cgi?number=T2654; "What's the difference between heart and soul?" Bible.org forum, accessed October 8, 2012, http://forum.bible.org/viewtopic.php?f=57&t=11075; "Heart and Mind: Emotion and Intellect," BibleFocus.net, March 15, 2009, http://biblefocus.net/notes/events/heart.html.
2. That's one of the definitions in *Merriam-Webster's Collegiate Dictionary*, 11th ed., s.v. "heart."
3. Ibid., "wellspring."
4. As in other specific stories in this book, Helen's name and some details of her story have been changed to protect her privacy.

CHAPTER 3: LESSONS FROM THE GREEN
1. Brent Kelley, "Fore," About.com Golf, accessed October 8, 2012, http://golf.about.com/cs/golfterms/g/bldef_fore.htm.

CHAPTER 4: THE PERFORMING HEART
1. The phrase "listen to your life" is one made famous by Frederick Buechner.
2. Jan Meyers, *Listening to Love: Responding to the Startling Voice of God* (Colorado Springs: WaterBrook Press, 2004), 52–53.
3. Brent Curtis and John Eldredge, *The Sacred Romance: Drawing Closer to the Heart of God* (Nashville: Thomas Nelson, 1997), 107–108.

CHAPTER 6: THE CONTROLLING HEART
1. See Spiros Zodhiates, ed., *Hebrew Greek Key Study Bible: King James Version*, 3rd ed., (Chattanooga, TN: AMG, 1986), Genesis 3:1.
2. Ibid.
3. Max Lucado, *Traveling Light: Releasing the Burdens You Were Never Intended to Bear* (Nashville: Thomas Nelson, 2001), 23.
4. Bill Kelly, *Enchanted*, directed by Kevin Lima (2007; Burbank, CA: Walt Disney Studios Home Entertainment, 2008), DVD.

CHAPTER 7: THE CRITICAL HEART
1. Brian Dannelly and Michael Urban, *Saved!*, directed by Brian Dannelly (Beverly Hills, CA: MGM Home Entertainment, 2004), DVD.
2. Philip Yancey, *Soul Survivor* (New York: Doubleday, 2001), 58.
3. Eryn Sun, "10 Quotes by John Stott throughout the Years," CP World, *Christian Post*, July 28, 2011, http://www.christianpost.com/news/john-stotts-words-throughout-the-ages-53021/.
4. Yancey, *Soul Survivor*, 55.

CHAPTER 8: THE SHAMED HEART
1. Beth Moore, *When Godly People Do Ungodly Things: Arming Yourself in the Age of Seduction* (Nashville: Broadman & Holman, 2002), 42.
2. "Anorexia & Bulimia," Quick Reference Counseling Keys Excerpt, Hope for the Heart Biblical Counseling Library, 2007–2009, http://www.hopefortheheart.org/pdfs/OLQR-pr-Anorexia%20&%20Bulimia.pdf.
3. Karen Kleinwort, "How Your Past Can Lead to Obesity," Divine Caroline, June 2011, http://www.divinecaroline.com/22175/115317-lead-obesity.
4. List quoted in its entirety from Tammy Maltby with Anne Christian Buchanan, *The God Who Sees You: Look to Him When You Feel Discouraged, Forgotten, or Invisible* (Colorado Springs: David C. Cook, 2012), 208.

CHAPTER 9: THE ANGRY HEART
1. "Unforgiveness: A Leading Cause of Cancer," Discover How Stress Causes Cancer and How to Heal Within, 2007–2012, http://www.alternative-cancer-care.com/Cancer_Forgiveness.html.
2. Walter Isaacson, *Steve Jobs* (New York: Simon & Schuster, 2011), 14–15.
3. Rick Warren, "Don't Be Reluctant to Show Mercy," *Daily Hope with Rick Warren* (blog), June 25, 2010, http://purposedriven.com/blogs/dailyhope/index.html?contentid=4619.

CHAPTER 10: THE FEARFUL HEART
1. Tamar E. Chansky, *Freeing Your Child from Anxiety: Powerful, Practical Solutions to Overcome Your Child's Fears, Worries, and Phobias* (New York:

Three Rivers Press, 2004), 22. I am indebted to what I learned in Dr. Chansky's book for much of this discussion of anxiety in childhood.

2. For a great description of this phenomenon, see Nancy Gibbs, "The Growing Backlash against Overparenting, *Time* online, November 30, 2009, http://www.time.com/time/magazine/article/0,9171,1940697,00 .html. See also Foster Cline and Jim Fay, *Parenting with Love and Logic*, rev. ed. (Colorado Springs, CO: NavPress, 2006).

3. This fact is widely reported, but one helpful source is Keith Krell, "'Fear Factor' (Genesis 15:1-21)," Bible.org, 2005, http://bible.org/seriespage/fear-factor-genesis-151-21.

4. Jan Meyers, *Listening to Love*, 106–107.

CHAPTER 11: THE WEARY HEART

1. "Secret Sauce: China's Rapid Growth Is Due Not Just to Heavy Investment, but Also to the World's Fastest Productivity Gains," *The Economist*, November 12, 2009, http://www.economist.com/node/14844987.

2. *The Jewish Study Bible* (Oxford: Oxford University Press, 2004), 1307.

3. Joyce Meyer, "Rest Awhile," Spiritual Life, CBN.com, accessed October 8, 2012, http://www.cbn.com/spirituallife/devotions/Meyer_RestAwhile.aspx.

4. Matthew Henry, *Matthew Henry Commentary on the Whole Bible*, Mark 2, BibleStudyTools.com, 2012, http://www.biblestudytools.com /commentaries/matthew-henry-complete/mark/2.html?p=5.

5. Joe Lieberman with David Klinghoffer, *The Gift of Rest: Rediscovering the Beauty of the Sabbath* (New York: Howard Books, 2011), ix.

CHAPTER 12: LIVING WITH A RECLAIMED HEART

1. C. S. Lewis, *The Four Loves*, reissue edition (New York: Houghton Mifflin Harcourt, 1991), 121.

About the Author

Denise Hildreth Jones has spent the last eight years writing fiction that has been hailed as both "smart and witty." Her ability to express the heart of the Southern voice has led to her being featured twice in *Southern Living* and receiving the accolades of readers and reviewers alike, but it is the simple joy of writing stories that keeps them coming.

Denise also founded the ministry Reclaiming Hearts, where she leads seasonal Bible studies and offers, with her husband, Reclaiming Your Heart weekend experiences that walk out the principles in this book on a deeper level.

Denise makes her home in Franklin, Tennessee, with her husband, five bonus children, and her dog. And on her days off, she will settle for a long walk with a friend or a good book and a Coca-Cola.

Visit Denise's websites at www.reclaiminghearts.com and www.denisehildrethjones.com.